MW00633948

Anti-Money Laudering and Combating Terrorist Financing for Financial Institutions

by

Ismail A. Odeh

DORRANCE PUBLISHING CO., INC.
PITTSBURGH, PENNSYLVANIA 15222

ISBN: 978-1-4349-0453-9
Printed in the United States of America

First Printing

For information or to order additional books, please write:
Dorrance Publishing Co., Inc.
701 Smithfield St.
Pittsburgh, Pennsylvania 15222
U.S.A.
1-800-788-7654
www.dorrancebookstore.com

Contents

To

The one and only one, my dearest wife.
Without her persistent encouragement and support, this accomplishment would not have been possible at all.

My sweetest children, for the inspiration of enduring love to write this book in hopes of a brighter and crimeless future.

Preface

In today's global markets, the attempts to use financial institutions to launder money and to be used as channels to finance terrorism is a major issue that is causing a great alarm in the international community and has led to the passage of stricter laws and regulations and increased penalties in many countries worldwide. The increasing problem has also spurred the formation of the Financial Action Task Force (FATF)[1], an inert governmental team comprised of thirty-two nations and two international organizations: the European Commission and the Gulf Cooperation Council, established to coordinate the global fight against money laundering and terrorist financing.

In an effort to better understand the scope of the problem, this book will define money laundering and terrorist financing, examine the various stages of money laundering, and demonstrate who controls the illegal funds circulating the globe.

---

[1] The Financial Action Task Force on money laundering (FATF) is an intergovernmental body whose purpose is the development and promotion of policies to combat money laundering. These policies aim to prevent such proceeds from being utilized in future criminal activities and from affecting legitimate economic activities. It currently consists of thirty-two countries and two international organizations. Its membership includes the major financial center countries of Europe, North America, and Asia. It is a multidisciplinary body dealing with money laundering and bringing together the policymaking power of legal, financial, and law enforcement experts.

In order to understand why nations care about this topic, this book will look at the size of the problem globally and the issues surrounding the collateral consequences of money laundering and terrorist financing at a macro geo-economic level.

More importantly, this book will examine why financial institutions should care in discussing the risks associated with reputation, regulatory, and the potential criminal consequences, both for the institution and the individual.

We will then look at some of the international initiatives undertaken to combat money laundering and the financing of terrorists in addition to highlighting some anti-money laundering laws in a number of countries.

The book will also highlight how money laundering occurs by examining several techniques during the various stages of the money laundering process. The reader will have an opportunity to see some examples that contain elements of money laundering cases.

The latter part of the book will address the policies, procedures, and programs financial institutions need to implement to minimize the risk of money laundering and terrorist financing in their businesses and the important role each one of their employees plays in achieving that goal. In addition, the latter part of the book provides a list of red flags (warning signs) that serve as indicators of abnormal and/or suspicious activities. The book then provides a self-assessment questionnaire, which should help countries and financial institutions to evaluate the effectiveness of their anti-money laundering and combating terrorist financing laws and regulations and their implementation.

The book establishes a set of governing policies and standards to protect financial institutions from being used to launder money and finance terrorism. I would, therefore, recommend this book to be read by all employees of financial institutions (banks, insurance companies, money exchangers, investment companies, brokerage firms, etc.), lawyers, and also, as a preparation and a defensive step, by all university students who are going for their banking and finance or legal degree.

Introduction

Money laundering and terrorism financing are two of the most serious and difficult risk issues facing financial institutions today. Financial institutions and their employees have been placed on the front lines in the fight against money laundering and terrorist financing and have to become the gatekeepers to the global financial system.

The risk of financial institutions being misused to facilitate and be channels to launder money and finance terrorism increases as financial institutions continue to expand around the globe. It is, therefore, of utmost importance that new, innovative, and effective ways of fighting money laundering and terrorist financing be developed and implemented.

Combating money laundering and terrorism financing should represent a significant investment for financial institutions and their employees' time. It should be a reflection of the commitment of senior management to ensure each employee understands his or her responsibility and role in the fight against money laundering and terrorism financing and has the appropriate training and tools to achieve that objective. The goal of senior management should be to ensure their financial institutions and businesses have effective and comprehensive anti-money laundering and terrorism financing programs tailored to the business in question and are responsive to the external environment. Such programs should define money laundering and the types of predicate crimes that constitute it.

Many recently enacted anti-money laundering and combating terrorist financing laws bring financial institutions to the front lines of the war on money laundering and terrorism. Under the requirements of the laws, financial institutions must play a direct role in protecting their countries and themselves by implementing methods to disrupt the funding of terrorists and money launderers.

In today's environment, it is no longer enough to know your customers, but it is rather know your customers better and better. As money launderers and terrorists perfect their techniques, widen their account networks, and increase the complexity of their transactions, financial institutions must depend on an anti-money laundering solution that is sophisticated enough to keep themselves one step ahead.

To meet the new requirements of the many laws, an anti-money laundering solution must be considered. It may be computerized or manual, taking into account the size and nature of the financial institution's operations and the available technology. If an automated solution is chosen, it must at least have data management, detection, tracking, and suspicious activities reporting mechanism.

Financial institutions must be proactive and vigilant in the battle against money laundering and terrorism financing. They must not allow themselves to be used for money laundering and terrorists financing activities or permit themselves to become violators of the laws of the countries where they do business.

What Is Money Laundering?

Money laundering is the process of integrating the proceeds of crime into the legitimate stream of financial commerce by masking its origin. It is a process of making illegitimate funds appear legitimate.

Money Laundering as a Crime

Most crimes are committed for money or some type of financial gain. Therefore, individuals committing crime need to engage in transactions with these funds to disguise the fact that the funds are derived from illegal activity. The funds must be laundered if they are to be secured and enjoyed. The underlying criminal (predicate) offence generates illegal proceeds. If there are transactions with these proceeds, this constitutes money laundering.

The Money Laundering Control Act, for example, first criminalized money laundering in the United States in 1986. Saudi Arabia, as another example, issued an anti-money laundering law in 2003, criminalizing money laundering and terrorism financing.

In most countries, money laundering is the proceeds related to many illicit activities including drug trafficking, corruption, embezzlement, wire and mail fraud, bribery, terrorist financing, racketeering, smuggling, etc. In the United States, e.g., there are now nearly 200 predicate crimes that constitute money laundering. Some of the illicit activities, which are identified as predicate crimes under the United States Money Laundering Control Act, can occur outside the United States.

Criminal organizations commingle proceeds from many crimes, and criminals act as brokers for funds unrelated to their own criminal activities. These trends make it more difficult to differentiate between drug related money laundering and other forms of illegal money movements.

Drug-related money laundering often supplies the working capital for other types of illicit activities, including financing terrorist groups (e.g. heroin trade in some countries).

The United States Patriot Act[2] (acronym for Uniting and Strengthening America by Providing Appropriate Tools Required to Intercept) also added foreign official corruption and certain foreign smuggling and export control violations to the United States list of predicate crimes.

Tax offences do not generally constitute a predicate offence for money laundering in most countries, with Mexico, however, a notable exception.

Many people often confuse money laundering with fraud. There are, however, differences between the two. Fraud is carrying out a scheme to obtain money or any form of property by means of false pretenses. When a financial institution experiences a fraud, it will incur a loss or disappearance of assets. When a financial institution is used to launder money, on the other hand, it will not experience a loss unless funds are seized or frozen by governments. Money laundering usually results in large quantities of illicit proceeds that need to be distanced from its source as quickly as possible in an undetected manner.

---

[2] A United States anti-money laundering law passed right after the September 11 events.

The Stages of Money Laundering Process

Generally speaking, money laundering process involves three stages:

Placement- The first stage involves the physical introduction of bulk cash into the financial system, typically accomplished through cash deposits and purchases of cash equivalent monetary instruments. At the placement stage, the funds are usually laundered relatively close to the underlying activity, often, but not in every case, in the country where the funds originate. The major exception to this would be bulk currency smuggling, which entails moving the physical cash proceeds to another country for placement.

Layering- The second phase involves separating the proceeds of criminal activity from their source through complex layers of transactions. The launderer seeks to separate the proceeds from the source through various complex layers of transactions. It typically involves more than one financial institution for obscuring the audit trail if more than one jurisdiction or country is involved. At this phase, the launderer may choose an offshore (placing assets outside of the entity's home country for three reasons: privacy, protection from lawsuits, and regulatory advantages) financial center, a large regional business center, or a world banking center, or any location that provides an adequate financial or business infrastructure. At this stage, the laundered funds may also only transit bank accounts at various locations where this can be done without leaving traces of their source or ultimate destination.

Integration- The final stage involves placing the laundered proceeds back into the economy in such a way that they reenter the financial system as apparently legitimate funds. During this phase, legitimate explanations are derived for the money launderer's wealth. In general, this is accomplished through schemes, such as real estate purchases, shell companies (companies that do not maintain a physical presence in any country), investments in securities, and other investments, in a way that the funds reenter financial institutions as legitimate funds. The funds thus become part of the legitimate funds making it so difficult to differentiate between legal and illegal funds.

We will explore some products and services that are utilized at each stage of the process later in the book.

Money Laundering Is a Major Global Problem

This is best illustrated by figures below that represent guesstimates by law enforcement around the globe:

➤ An estimated 900 billion to 1 trillion US dollars of illicit funds circulating worldwide
➤ Approximately 500 to 600 billion US dollars associated with the drug trade
➤ About 300 billion US dollars associated with United States drug sales
➤ Other target countries are nations with a high gross national product and high per capita income.

By its very nature, money laundering occurs outside the range of economic statistics. Nevertheless, as with other aspects of underground economic activity, rough estimates have been put forward to give some sense of the scale of the problem.

Michael Camdesus, former director of the International Monetary Fund (IMF)[3], for example, has stated that the aggregate size of money laundering in the world could be somewhere between 2 and 5 percent of the world's gross domestic product.

Using 1996 statistics, these percentages would indicate that money laundering ranged between USD 590 billion and USD

---

[3] The IMF is an international organization of 184 member countries. It was established to promote international monetary cooperation, exchange stability, and orderly exchange arrangements; to foster economic growth and high levels of employment; and to provide temporary financial assistance to countries to help ease balance of payments adjustment.

1.5 trillion. The lower figure is roughly equivalent to the value of the total output of an economy the size of Spain.

It has been estimated that the amount of money laundered in the Arab world is about 100 billion dollars a year, most of it in the Gulf States.

Who Controls the Illegal Funds Circulating the Globe?

Mafia groups (United States Mafia, Italian Mafia, Asian Triads, Russian Mafia, Latin American drug cartels, etc.) represent transnational organized crimes and operate freely beyond geographic borders, much as global corporations do.

In her book *Crime Without Frontiers,* journalist Claire Sterling states "the birth of a worldwide Mafia International is a reality. The collapse of the Soviet empire, opening new markets of vast potential, has brought the big crime groups of the east and the west together. The Sicilian and American mafias in particular are now working with their counterparts in Eastern Europe and the former Soviet Union, operating across and beyond Europe and the United States. Their leaders have met at summits, three times in as many years: in Warsaw in 1991, in Prague in 1992, and in Berlin in 1993. There, they agreed to apply strategic planning and market development policies for the new emerging free markets, to program legitimate investments much as corporations do, and to develop and expand extremely illegal activities besides. The latter mostly involved trafficking in narcotics, conventional arms, and weapons of mass destruction."

Money Laundering vs. Terrorism

While most criminals engage in crime for profit, terrorists, on the other hand, engage in crime for purpose, usually publicity and political purpose.

The primary objective of terrorism according to one definition[4] is to "intimidate a population or to compel a government or an international organization to do or abstain from doing any act." According to the United States Federal Bureau of Investigation's (FBI) definition, "terrorism is the unlawful use of force or violence against persons or property to intimidate or coerce a government, the civilian population, or any segment thereof, in furtherance of political or social objectives." In contrast, financial gain is generally the objective of other types of criminal activity. In other words, terrorists differ from other criminal networks in the motive behind crimes.

Funding of Terrorism

Terrorist organizations require financial support in order to achieve their aims, and a successful terrorist organization, like any criminal organization, is therefore one that is able to build and maintain an effective financial infrastructure. Terrorists and their organizations need finance for a wide variety or purposes such as

---

[4] International Convention for the Suppression of Financing of Terrorism, December 9, 1999

recruitment, training, travel, materials, and safe haven protection. Tracking, intercepting, and strangling the flow of funds are vital elements in the global effort against terrorism. The intelligence that can be gained into terrorist networks through knowledge of their financial transactions and dealings is vital in protecting national and international security and upholding the integrity of national and international financial systems.

Terrorists often control funds from a variety of sources around the world and employ increasingly sophisticated techniques to move those funds between jurisdictions. Funds that are not required immediately can be invested in a variety of products and assets. To achieve their objectives, they require the services of skilled professionals such as bankers, accountants, and lawyers.

Terrorism, therefore, like other criminal activities, must develop sources of funding and a means of laundering those funds. Some funding by terrorists may include criminal acts; in this way, they may appear similar to ordinary criminal organizations, while other funding includes legal activities. Much of the role that legal monies play in the support of terrorism seems to vary according to the terrorist group and whether its source of funds is in the same geographic location as its terrorist acts.

As previously stated, the key difference between terrorist groups and other criminal groups is the reliance on legally generated sources of income which makes detection of such activities much more of a challenge, as well as the fact that terrorism requires very little money (attacks on World Trade Center and the Pentagon, for example, are estimated to have cost a little more than half a million dollars).

Thus, the amounts that terrorists seek to disguise are substantially less compared to that laundered by organized crime and drug kingpins. It is the latter for which anti-money laundering laws and regulations were established, and, it has been suggested these may not be useful in detecting terrorists financing. Let's examine the means of terrorist financing in more details.

Origins of Terrorism Financial Support

As previously mentioned, terrorism financing includes illegal revenue generating activities, as well as legally generated sources of funds.

Experts generally agree that terrorist financing comes from two primary sources. The first source of funds of terrorist organizations is income derived directly from various illegal revenue generating activities. As with criminal organizations, a terrorist group's income may be derived directly from crime or other unlawful activities. A terrorist group in a particular region may support itself through kidnapping and extortion. In this scenario, ransoms are paid to retrieve hostages, along with a revolutionary tax (a euphemism for protection money) demanded of businesses, provide needed financial resources but also play a secondary role as one other means of intimidating the target population. Besides kidnapping and extortion, terrorist groups may engage in large-scale smuggling, various types of fraud, thefts and robbery, and narcotics trafficking.

The second source is the financial support provided by states or organizations with large enough infrastructures to collect and then make funds available to the terrorist organization. Several rogue nations have allegedly provided material assistance, financial support, or other resources to terrorists. An individual with sufficient financial means may also provide funding to terrorists. The so-called State-sponsored terrorism has declined in recent years, according to some experts, increasingly replaced by other types of backing.

Sources of terrorist funding or financing include legally generated sources of funds. Such legally generated sources of income include donations from wealthy donors, community solicitation and fundraising appeals in the name of charitable, relief, or religious organizations, and proceeds derived from legitimate commercial enterprises (terrorist groups earn profits from commercial enterprises they own). This makes detection of such activities much more of a challenge. Community solicitation and fundraising is one of the most effective means of raising funds to support terrorism. Often, such fundraising is carried out in the name of organizations having the status of charitable or relief organization. Some members of the community are led to believe they are giving for a good cause. In many cases, the charities to which the donations are given are in fact legitimate in that they do engage in some of the work they purport to carry out. Most members of the organization, however, have no knowledge that a portion of the funds raised by the charity is being diverted to terrorist causes.

For instance, the supporters from a terrorist movement from one country may carry out ostensibly legal activities in another country to obtain financial resources. The movement's supporters raise these funds by infiltrating and taking control of institutions within the immigrant community of the second country. Some of the specific fundraising methods might include collection of membership dues and/or subscriptions, sale of publications, speaking tours, door-to-door solicitation, and appeals to wealthy members of the community.

In the United States, e.g. in 2001, the government seized the assets of three Muslim foundations for allegedly providing financial support to terrorist groups. The three charitable organizations—Global Relief Foundation, Benevolence International Foundation, and Holy Land Foundation—are all incorporated in the United States and receive tax exempt status from the Internal Revenue Service (IRS). All three groups alleged that their property was taken without just compensation in violations of the Fifth Amendment, and their assets seized in violation of the Forth Amendment of the United States Constitution. Complicating the issue is a tenet of the Muslim faith, Zakat, which holds that it is preferable for Muslims to make anonymous charitable donations.

From a technical perspective, the methods used by terrorists and their associates to generate funds from illegal sources differ little from those used by traditional criminal organizations. Although it would seem logical that funding from legitimate sources would not need to be laundered, there is nevertheless need for terrorist groups to obscure or disguise links between it and its legitimate funding sources. It follows that terrorist groups must find ways to launder these funds without drawing the attention of authorities. In examining terrorist-related financial activity, the Financial Action Task Force (FATF) experts have concluded that terrorists and their support organizations generally use the same methods as criminal groups to launder funds. Such methods include:

1. Currency transport: cash couriered by operatives is difficult to track because there is no paper trail.
2. Traditional financial institutions: The international nature of most foreign terrorist groups forces them to rely on banks and other financial institutions.
3. Islamic Banks: banks that operate in line with Islamic law, which prohibits the payment of interest and certain other activities, have proliferated throughout Africa, Asia, and the Middle East since the middle 1970s. In most instances, these banks simply are not required to adhere to a wide range of regulations normally imposed on commercial banks. Islamic banks are often not subject to any regulatory and supervisory scrutiny by bank regulators, and thus, do not undergo periodic bank examinations or inspections. While these banks may voluntarily comply with banking regulations, in particular anti-money laundering guidelines, there is often no control mechanism to ensure such compliance. Some of the largest Islamic financial institutions now operate investment houses in Europe and elsewhere.
4. Moneychangers: Moneychangers play a major role in transferring funds in Asia, the Americas, the Middle East, and other regions. Their presence is largest in countries where cash is an accepted means to finalize business deals and where large numbers of expatriates work to remit funds to families abroad.
5. Underground bankers: commonly referred to as alternative remittance systems, such as the *Hawala*[5] that is prevalent throughout Asia and the Middle East.

---

[5] The word "Hawala" is Hindi meaning trust or exchange. It is often used in relation with the word Hundi that stands for bill of exchange. *Hawala* is an unofficial alternative remittance and money exchange system enabling the transfer of funds without their actual physical move. *Hawala* works as follows: Individual brokers or operators, known as *Hawaladars*, collect funds at one end of the payment chain and others distribute the funds at the other. For example, an expatriate working in America who wants to send money back to his family in India turns to a moneylender or trader with contacts in both countries giving him the money. The trader calls a trusted partner in the home country who delivers the amount to the family, minus a commission. For identification and details of the trade, often a code is used. The two traders settle accounts either through reciprocal remittances, trade invoice manipulations, gold and precious gem smuggling, the conventional banking system, or by physical movement of currency.

Why Should Nations Care?

To answer this question, we need to look at corruption and its relationship to money laundering. When transnational organized crimes control billions of dollars, they have the ability to corrupt public officials (e.g. the policeman on the street up to the president). Corruption is a major problem in many countries in the world, including the most industrial nations, like the United States and the United Kingdom. If organized crime can buy public officials, they undermine the political integrity of the country and infuse illegal capital into the economy, which is a destabilizing economic factor.

Corruption of private individuals (e.g., bankers, brokers, accountants, lawyers, and other white-collar professionals) is also a problem. Launderers target these people since they are useful in the laundering process.

Terrorism has also been on the rise in the past ten years. Nearly every country has some sort of terrorist group operating within it (e.g., *Euskadi ta Askatasuna*, which means Basque Fatherland and Liberty, better known as ETA in Spain, Irish Republican Army in United Kingdom, Shining Path in Peru, and Partia Karkaren Kurdistan in Turkey). Government sources indicate that legitimate businesses, illegitimate business (such as corruption and drug trafficking), donations from wealthy individuals, fake charities, etc. are among the sources of terrorist financing.

Terrorists and transnational organized crime have a symbiotic relationship and engage not only in narcotics trafficking but also traffic in illegal arms. We are not talking about handguns, but potentially weapons that have been pillaged out of the arsenals of the former Soviet Union and are for sale on the world market. The combination of public corruption, increased terrorist activity, and illegal arms trafficking is an explosive combination.

Nations care about money laundering because they care about their political and economic stability. This is an issue of survival.

Why Should Financial Institutions Care?

There is a significant risk to the reputation of financial institutions, as well as franchise risk due to the negative press and legal and regulatory penalties. Any negative press contributes to the public's perceptions regarding the banking institution, the banking industry as a whole, and the government's inability to control money laundering. It contributes to the loss of confidence in the integrity of the institution. Below are some examples of risks some financials institutions faced:

➢ Bank of Credit and Commerce International (BCCI) forfeited fifteen million dollars and lost its Florida Bank charter; an avalanche of negative media attention and public scrutiny resulted in BCCI's demise.
➢ American Express paid fifty million dollars to the United States Government, and two of its senior bankers received significant jail terms in a money laundering prosecution related to private bank activity.

This was the first time the theory of willful blindness was used in a money laundering prosecution. The bankers did not actually know their client was involved in laundering money for a Mexican drug cartel, but they did not follow the Know Your Customer (KYC) [6] procedures established at the time and ignored

---

[6] KYC is discussed in full details in a later section.

several warning signs that should have alerted them to suspicious activity; therefore, they were held to know under United States law.

Part of the fallout of negative media attention with regard to money laundering is increased regulatory supervision and scrutiny and loss of reputation in the worldwide community, which would be harmful to any corporate franchise.

International Initiatives to Combat Money Laundering

United Nations Initiatives

In recognizing the global enormity of money laundering and the financing of terrorism, the United Nations has made significant efforts to the fight against money laundering and the combat of terrorist financing. The United Nations has created a program called Global Program against Money Laundering (GPML), which has been a key instrument of the United Nations Office on Drugs and Crime (UNODC) in this mission. Through this global program, the United Nations helps member states introduce legislation against money laundering and develop and maintain the mechanisms to combat this crime. This program supports anti-money laundering policy development, monitors and analyses the problems and responses, raises public awareness about money laundering, and acts as a coordinator of joint anti-money laundering initiatives by the United Nations with other international organizations.

The United Nations has thus far issued the following resolutions in its efforts to fight and combat money laundering and the financing of terrorists and force its member nations to take and enforce similar legislations:

- United Nations Convention against Illicit Traffic in Narcotic Drugs and Psychotropic Substances, 1988
- International Convention for the Suppression of the Financing of Terrorism Preamble, United Nations, 1999
- United Nations Resolution 1373 (2001): Adopted by the Security Council at its 4385th meeting, on 28 September 2001
- Resolution 1390 (2002): Adopted by the Security Council at its 4452nd meeting, on 16 January 2002

The full details of the above stated resolutions are presented in Appendix II.

The International Money Laundering Information Network

In 1996, the world's leading international organizations involved in the fight against money laundering and in the combating of financing of terrorism agreed to produce a common Internet website where information could be shared among national and international anti-money laundering agencies. The International Money Laundering Information Network (IMoLIN) was the outcome of this agreement.

IMoLIN is an Internet-based network assisting governments, organizations, and individuals in the fight against money laundering and the financing of terrorism. IMoLIN has been developed with the cooperation of the world's leading anti-money laundering organizations. Included therein is a database on legislation and regulation throughout the world (AMLID), an electronic library, and a calendar of events in the anti-money laundering / countering the financing of terrorism fields. Please be advised that certain aspects of IMoLIN are secured and therefore not available for public use. The key features of the IMoLIN system are:

- The Anti-Money Laundering International Database (AMLID) - a compendium of analyses of anti-money laundering laws and regulations, including two general classes of money laundering control measures: domestic laws and international cooperation, as well as information about national contacts and authorities. AMLID is a secure, multi-lingual database and is an important reference tool for law enforcement officers involved in cross-jurisdictional work;

- A reference section that contains details of the United Nation's latest research, a bibliography, and abstracts of the best new research from other sources;
- A click-on map that takes users to regional lists of national legislation, together with links to the web sites of related regional organizations and financial intelligence units (FIUs). Eventually, this section will contain the full text of all national anti-money laundering legislation throughout the world;
- The full text of the United Nations model legislation on money laundering for common law and civil law systems;
- A calendar of events that lists current training events and conferences at the national, regional, and international level and;
- A links section that takes users to other relevant sites concerned with the fight against money laundering.

The Global Program against Money Laundering

The Global Program against Money Laundering (GPML) was established in1997 in response to a mandate arising from the 1988 Convention under which member states were required to criminalize money laundering related to the proceeds of illicit trafficking in drugs and to put legal frameworks in place to facilitate the identification, freezing, seizing, and confiscation of the proceeds of crime.

The role of GPML was strengthened by the Political Declaration and the measures countering money laundering (resolution S-20/4 D of 10 June 1998) adopted by the General Assembly at its twentieth special session, under which member states were called upon to put a number of specific measures in place, in particular, with reference to the activities of financial institutions. UNODC was specifically requested to continue its work within the framework of GPML. Under the United Nations Convention against Transnational Organized Crime (General Assembly resolution 55/25, annex I, of 15 November 2000), the definition of money laundering will be expanded to include the proceeds of all serious crimes, and legal force will be given to a number of issues addressed in the Political Declaration. Those issues include the requirement to adopt legal and administrative measures to regulate financial activities and to facilitate the detection, investigation, and prosecution of money laundering.

Member states need to establish legislative frameworks to criminalize the laundering of money derived from serious crimes and to prevent, detect, investigate, and prosecute money laundering. They also need to establish effective financial and regulatory regimes to deny criminals and their illicit funds access to national and international financial systems. They further need to implement law enforcement measures to provide tools against money laundering criminals, including their extradition, as well as effective information-sharing mechanisms.

Objective

The objective is to strengthen the ability of member states to fight money laundering and to assist them in depriving persons of the proceeds of their criminal activity.

Strategy

GPML continues to fulfill its mandate principally through technical cooperation and research. Technical cooperation will focus on assisting legal, financial, and law enforcement authorities in developing the necessary infrastructure to fight money laundering. Specific initiatives are built around awareness raising, institution building, and training. The research activity will continue to focus on work that adds to the body of information on contemporary issues relevant to money laundering, the maintenance and improvement of relevant databases, the analysis of data on specific aspects of money laundering, and the provision of logistic support for technical cooperation activities at the country level. GPML will seek to ensure that member states create legal frameworks and administrative machinery required to give effect to relevant money laundering provisions contained in the 1988 Convention and generally to meet accepted international anti-money laundering standards. It will also seek to ensure that member states introduce the measures highlighted in the Political Declaration and the measures countering money laundering adopted at the twentieth special session.

GPML will continue to provide the following principal types of assistance to member states: initiatives to raise levels of awareness among key persons in both the government and financial sectors about money laundering, its potential negative impact on an economy and the measures necessary to combat it; drafting and reviewing money laundering legislation and legislative amendments; developing and updating model legislation on money laundering and proceeds of crime in coordination with the UNODC Legal Assistance Program; establishing institutional machinery required to give effect to the legislation, in particular, the development of financial intelligence units in the context of the GPML working relationship with the Egmont Group; training for legal, judicial, law enforcement, and financial regulatory authorities, as well as for relevant private sector officials to enhance their capacity to undertake their respective roles within an anti-money laundering infrastructure; databases and analysis of information that can be used by member states and organizations involved in the fight against money laundering; developing and maintaining strategic relationships with the Commonwealth Secretariat, the Egmont Group, the Financial Action Task Force (FATF), the International Monetary Fund, Interpol, the World Bank, the World Customs Organization, FATF-style Regional Bodies (the Asia Pacific Group on Money Laundering (APG), the Caribbean Financial Action Task Force (C-FATF), the Inter-American Drug Abuse Control Commission (CICAD) of the Organization of American States (OAS), the Eastern and Southern Africa Anti-Money Laundering Group (ESAAMLG), and the Council of Europe Select Committee of Experts on the Evaluation of Anti-Money Laundering Measures (PC-E-RV)). In so doing, GPML will broaden the range and diversity of resources on which it can draw to assist in undertaking its work and avoid duplication in the delivery of technical assistance.

GPML will produce studies on various aspects of money laundering and manage a web site, the International Money Laundering Information Network (IMoLIN) and the associated

Anti Money Laundering International Database (AMLID) on behalf of a number of international organizations involved in the fight against money laundering.

Money laundering is a dynamic field, frequently subject to changes in techniques, technology, jurisprudence, and policy approaches (both at the national and international level). Activities of GPML will naturally continue to be structured and altered as necessary to take account of current circumstances; and thus, to remain responsive to the changing needs of member states and the international community.

External factors that can impact the work of GPML include initiatives undertaken by other multilateral organizations. The level of political commitment to implement necessary measures at the national level and the effectiveness of the public sector in implementing changes are also important variables. So, too, is the responsiveness of the private sector, in particular that of financial institutions and providers of professional services.

GPML will be subject to an external evaluation during the biennium to assess outcomes and impact.

The Formation of the Financial Action Task Force (FAFT)

The Financial Action Task Force on money laundering (FATF) is an inter-governmental body whose purpose is the development and promotion of policies, both at national and international levels, to combat money laundering. As stated in its website, "FATF was established by the G-7 Summit held in Paris in 1989 in response to mounting concern over money laundering. Recognizing the threat posed to the banking system and to financial institutions, the G-7 heads of state or government and president of the European Commission convened the Task Force from the G-7 member states, the European Commission, and eight other countries.

"The Task Force was given the responsibility of examining money laundering techniques and trends, reviewing the actions already taken at a national or international level, and setting out the measures that still needed to be taken to combat money laundering. In April 1990, less than one year after its creation, the FATF issued a report containing a set of Forty Recommendations, which provide a comprehensive plan of action needed to fight against money laundering.

"During 1991 and 1992, the FATF expanded its membership from the original sixteen to twenty-eight members. In 2000, the FATF expanded to thirty-one members. In 2003, it acquired thirty-three members, and in 2007, it expanded to its current thirty-four members. For more, see FATF Members and Observers. The FATF has continued to examine the methods used to launder criminal proceeds and has completed two rounds of mutual evaluations of its member countries and jurisdictions. A third round of mutual evaluations has commenced. For more on mutual evaluations, see Monitoring the Implementation of the Forty Recommendations. It has also updated the Forty Recommendations to reflect the changes which have occurred in money laundering and has sought to encourage other countries around the world to adopt anti-money laundering measures.

"In 2001, the development of standards in the fight against terrorist financing was added to the mission of the FATF."

The Task Force is a policymaking body which works to generate the necessary political will to bring about national legislative and regulatory reforms to combat money laundering. It is considered the premier multilateral body in combating money laundering.

Members of the FATF include thirty-four countries and jurisdictions including the major financial center countries of Europe, North and South America, and Asia, as well as the European Commission and the Gulf Cooperation Council.

FATF works closely with other international bodies involved in combating money laundering. While the Organization for Economic Co-operation and Development (OECD)[7] houses its secretariat, FATF is not part of the organization. However, when the efforts of the OECD and FATF complement each other, such as on bribery and corruption or the functioning of the international financial system, the two cooperate.

The objectives of FATF are to enlarge its membership, develop credible and effective FATF-style regional bodies, and increase cooperation with relevant international organizations.

---

[7] The OECD groups thirty member countries sharing a commitment to democratic government and the market economy. With active relationships with some seventy other countries, Non-Government Organizations and civil societies, it has a global reach. Best known for its publications and its statistics, its work covers economic and social issues from macroeconomics, to trade, education, development and science and innovation.

The FATF team drew up Forty Recommendations[8] in 1990 (Appendix III highlights the full forty recommendations) as an initiative to combat the misuse of the financial system by persons laundering drug money. In 1996, based upon experience gained and reflecting the changes that had occurred in the money laundering problem, the application was extended beyond drug trafficking to serious crimes. The recommendations have now been endorsed by over 100 countries and are widely accepted as the leading anti-money laundering standard. The Forty Recommendations for banking practices in member nations were issued to impede money laundering. There are three basic categories significant for financial institutions:

➢ Establishment of a large cash transaction reporting or recording system
➢ Creation of a methodology for interacting with financial institutions regulators and the local law enforcement concerning suspicious transactions, and
➢ Establishment of Know Your Customer and Enhanced Due Diligence policies and procedures

FATF is also responsible for conducting the evaluations of non-member nations' compliance with the Forty Recommendations and has designated a number of countries and territories as Non-Cooperative with international money laundering standards.

---

[8] These are the measures, which the Task Force has agreed to implement, and which all countries are encouraged to adopt. The Recommendations were originally drawn up in 1990 and in 1996 the forty Recommendations were revised. These Forty Recommendations set out the basic framework for Anti-money laundering efforts and they are designed to be of universal application. They cover the criminal justice system and law enforcement, the financial system and its regulation, and international cooperation.

FATF Initiatives on the Financing of Terrorism

The international consensus to fight terrorism has never been stronger. The international community is equipping itself with increasingly more effective tools to respond to terrorist financing.

During a Plenary session, FATF agreed to and issued new international standards to combat terrorist financing which calls upon all countries to adopt and implement. Implementing these Eight Special Recommendations and a ninth recommendation added in early 2005 (please refer to appendix III for a summary of Nine Special Recommendations) will deny terrorists and their supporters' access to the international financial system.

In March 2001, FATF issued guidance notes on the Eight Special Recommendations on terrorist financing adopted by the FATF in October 2001. This guidance is meant to assist non-FATF members in understanding some of the concepts contained in the Eight Special Recommendations and serve as a guide to jurisdictions attempting to fill in and submit the FATF self-assessment questionnaire on terrorist financing. The guidance should help countries in many areas such as criminalizing money laundering, designating terrorist financing as a predicate offence for money laundering, confiscating assets, reporting suspicious transactions linked to terrorism, international cooperation, alternative remittance systems, and non-profit organizations.

A major priority of the FATF during 2001 and 2002 was the implementation of its plan of action to counter terrorist financing, which includes a self-assessment process for all its members on their anti-terrorist financing measures. Prior to September 11, 2001, member countries Japan and Canada had not criminalized terrorist financing. Since the creation of the Eight Special Recommendations, FATF members have been working quickly to come into compliance. FATF will continue to strive for full compliance of these recommendations, both with its own membership and globally.

In keeping with its commitment to global compliance, a voluntary self-assessment process for all other countries of the world was also launched on the same basis as for the FATF members, and FATF has so far received more than fifty responses. FATF will work to ensure that countries that have not yet replied to the questionnaire do so in a timely manner. FATF has established a working group to identify, based on the replies to the self-assessment questionnaire, countries that lack appropriate measures to counter terrorist financing for follow-up assessment and/or technical assistance by the International Monetary Fund, World Bank,[9] and the United Nations. The recommendations are summarized below:

1. Each country should take immediate steps to ratify and fully implement the 1999 United Nations International Convention for the Suppression of the Financing of Terrorism. Countries should also immediately implement the United Nations resolutions relating to the prevention and suppression of the financing of terrorist acts, particularly United Nations Security Council Resolution 1373.

2. Each country should criminalize the financing of terrorism, terrorist acts, and terrorist organizations. Countries should ensure such offences are designated as money laundering predicate offences.

3. Each country should implement measures to freeze without delay funds or other assets of terrorists and those who finance terrorism and terrorist organizations in accordance with the United Nations resolutions relating to the prevention and suppression of the financing of terrorist acts. Each country should also adopt and implement measures, including legislative ones, which would enable the competent authorities to seize and confiscate property that is the proceeds of, or

---

[9] The World Bank is one of the United Nations' specialized agencies, and is made up of 184 member countries. These countries are jointly responsible for how the institution is financed and how its money is spent. Along with the rest of the development community, the World Bank centers its efforts on reaching the Millennium Development Goals, agreed to by UN members in 2000 and aimed at sustainable poverty reduction. The World Bank is the name that has come to be used for the International Bank for Reconstruction and Development (IBRD) and the International Development Association (IDA). Together, these organizations provide low interest loans, interest free credit, and grants to developing countries.

used in, or intended or allocated for use in, the financing of terrorism, terrorist acts, or terrorist organizations.

4. If financial institutions, or other businesses or entities subject to anti-money laundering obligations, suspect or have reasonable grounds to suspect that funds are linked or related to, or are to be used for terrorism, terrorist acts, or by terrorist organizations, they should be required to report promptly their suspicions to the competent authorities.

5. Each country should afford another country, based on a treaty, arrangement, or other mechanism for mutual legal assistance or information exchange, the greatest possible measure of assistance in connection with criminal, civil enforcement, and administrative investigations, inquiries, and proceedings relating to the financing of terrorism, terrorist acts, and terrorist organizations. Countries should also take all possible measures to ensure they do not provide safe havens for individuals charged with the financing of terrorism, terrorist acts, or terrorist organizations and should have procedures in place to extradite, when possible, such individuals.

6. Each country should take measures to ensure persons or legal entities, including agents, who provide a service for the transmission of money or value, including transmission through an informal money or value transfer system or network, should be licensed or registered and subject to all FATF Recommendations that apply to banks and non-bank financial institutions. Each country should ensure persons or legal entities that carry out this service illegally are subject to administrative, civil, or criminal sanctions.

7. Countries should take measures to require financial institutions, including money remitters, to include accurate and meaningful originator information (name, address, and account number) on funds transfers and related messages that are sent, and the information should remain with the transfer or related message through the payment chain. Countries should take measures to ensure financial institutions, including money remitters, conduct enhanced scrutiny of and monitor for suspicious activity funds transfers that do not

contain complete originator information (name, address, and account number).

8. Countries should review the adequacy of laws and regulations that relate to entities that can be abused for the financing of terrorism. Non-profit organizations are particularly vulnerable, and countries should ensure they couldn't be misused:

> By terrorist organizations posing as legitimate entities;
> To exploit legitimate entities as conduits for terrorist financing, including for the purpose of escaping asset freezing measures; and
> To conceal or obscure the clandestine diversion of funds intended for legitimate purposes to terrorist organizations.

9. Countries should have measures in place to detect the physical cross-border transportation of currency and bearer negotiable instruments, including a declaration system or other disclosure obligation. Countries should ensure their competent authorities have the legal authority to stop or restrain currency or bearer negotiable instruments suspected to be related to terrorist financing or money laundering or that are falsely declared or disclosed.

Other Major Initiatives:

United States House and Senate and the United States Administration

Prior to September 11, 2001, there were already a number of legislative proposals in the United States House and Senate, and the United States administration was hinting at enhancing prosecutorial and regulatory resources to fight money laundering. The face of money laundering compliance has been changed forever since September 11, 2001. The United States Patriot Act, for instance, makes the financial war on terrorism a top priority, and financial institutions are in it for the long haul. This has fostered a greater spirit of cooperation between the public and private sectors.

The Wolfsberg Group Initiative

The Wolfsberg Group, an association of twelve global banks, aims to develop financial services industry principles for *Know Your Customer, Anti-Money Laundering and Combating Terrorist Financing* policies. The group was established in 2000 in Wolfsberg, Switzerland, to draft anti-money laundering guidelines for the private banking sector. In October of 2000, the group published its *Anti-Money Laundering Principles for Private Banking Sector.*

Subsequently in 2001 and in January 2002 (after the events of September eleventh), the group published its *Statement on the Financing of Terrorism*, and it also published its Anti-*Money Laundering Principles for Correspondent Banking* in November 2002. In 2004, the group focused on the development of a due diligence model for financial institutions, thereby fulfilling one of the recommendations made in the *Correspondent Banking Principles*.

During 2005 and early 2006, the group of banks actively worked on providing guidance with regard to a number of banking activities where principles had yet to be fully drafted by lawmakers or regulators. These activities developed guidelines for a Risk Based Approach for Managing Money Laundering Risks and AML Guidance for Mutual Funds and Other Pooled Investment Vehicles. In early 2007, the group issued a *Statement against Corruption* which describes the role of the Group and financial institutions in support of international efforts to combat corruption. The group's *Anti-Money Laundering and Combating the Financing of Terrorism* initiatives are shown below:

Global Anti-Money Laundering Guidelines for Private Banking, Wolfsberg1 AML Principles, (first revision, May 2002)

The following major international private banks have agreed to the following principles as important global guidance for sound business conduct in international private banking:

- ABN AMRO Bank N.V.
- Bank of Tokyo-Mitsubishi Ltd.
- Barclays Bank
- Citigroup
- Credit Suisse Group
- Deutsche Bank AG
- Goldman Sachs
- HSBC
- J.P. Morgan Private Bank
- Santander Central Hispano
- Société Générale
- UBS AG

Acknowledgement

The banks collaborated with a team from Transparency International who invited two international experts to participate: Stanley Morris and Prof. Mark Pieth. Transparency International and the experts regard the principles as an important step in the fight against money laundering, corruption, and other related serious crimes.

Wolfsberg AML Principles

The following guidelines are understood to be appropriate for private banking relationships. Guidelines for other market segments may differ. It is recognized that the establishment of policies and procedures to adhere to these guidelines is the responsibility of management.

A. Client acceptance: general guidelines

General

Bank policy will be to prevent the use of its worldwide operations for criminal purposes. The bank will endeavor to accept only those clients whose sources of wealth and funds can be reasonably established to be legitimate. The primary responsibility for this lies with the private banker who sponsors the client for acceptance. Mere fulfillment of internal review procedures does not relieve the private banker of this basic responsibility.

Identification

The bank will take reasonable measures to establish the identity of its clients and beneficial owners and will only accept clients when this process has been completed.

Client

- Natural persons: identity will be established to the bank's satisfaction by reference to official identity papers or such other evidence as may be appropriate under the circumstances.
- Corporations, partnerships, foundations: the bank will receive documentary evidence of the due organization and existence.
- Trusts: the bank will receive appropriate evidence of formation and existence along with identity of the trustees.
- Identification documents must be current at the time of opening.

Beneficial owner

Beneficial ownership must be established for all accounts. Due diligence must be done on all principal beneficial owners identified in accordance with the following principles:

- Natural persons: when the account is in the name of an individual, the private banker must establish whether the client is acting on his/her own behalf. If doubt exists, the bank will establish the capacity in which and on whose behalf the account holder is acting.
- Legal entities: where the client is a company, such as a private investment company, the private banker will understand the structure of the company sufficiently to determine the provider of funds, principal owner(s) of the shares, and those who have control over the funds, e.g., the directors and those with the power to give direction to the directors of the company. With regard to other shareholders, the private banker will make a reasonable judgment as to the need for further due diligence. This principle applies regardless of whether the share capital is in registered or bearer form.
- Trusts: when the client is a trustee, the private banker will understand the structure of the trust sufficiently to determine the provider of funds (e.g. settler), those who have control over the funds (e.g. trustees), and any persons or entities who have the power to remove the trustees. The private banker

will make a reasonable judgment as to the need for further due diligence.

- Unincorporated associations: the above principles apply to unincorporated associations.
- The bank will not permit the use of its internal non-client accounts (sometimes referred to as "concentration" accounts) to prevent association of the identity of a client with the movement of funds on the client's behalf, i.e., the bank will not permit the use of such internal accounts in a manner that would prevent the bank from appropriately monitoring the client's account activity.

Accounts held in the name of money managers and similar intermediaries

The private banker will perform due diligence on the intermediary and establish that the intermediary has a due diligence process for its clients, or a regulatory obligation to conduct such due diligence, that is satisfactory to the bank.

Powers of attorney/Authorized signers

When the holder of a power of attorney or another authorized signer is appointed by a client, it is generally sufficient to do due diligence on the client.

Practices for walk-in clients and electronic banking relationships

A bank will determine whether walk-in clients or relationships initiated through electronic channels require a higher degree of due diligence prior to account opening. The bank will specifically address measures to satisfactorily establish the identity of non-face-to-face customers.

Due diligence

It is essential to collect and record information covering the following categories:

- Purpose and reasons for opening the account
- Anticipated account activity
- Source of wealth (description of the economic activity which has generated the net worth)
- Estimated net worth
- Source of funds (description of the origin and the means of transfer for monies that are accepted for the account opening)
- References or other sources to corroborate reputation information where available.
- Unless other measures reasonably suffice to do the due diligence on a client (e.g. favorable and reliable references), a client will be met prior to account opening.

Numbered or alternate name accounts

Numbered or alternate name accounts will only be accepted if the bank has established the identity of the client and the beneficial owner. These accounts must be open to a level of scrutiny by the bank's appropriate control layers equal to the level of scrutiny applicable to other client accounts.

Offshore jurisdictions

Risks associated with entities organized in offshore jurisdictions are covered by due diligence procedures laid out in these guidelines.

Oversight responsibility

There will be a requirement that all new clients and new accounts be approved by at least one person other than the private banker.

B. Client acceptance: situations requiring additional diligence / attention

General

In its internal policies, the bank must define categories of persons whose circumstances warrant additional diligence. This will typically be the case when the circumstances are likely to pose a higher than average risk to a bank.

Indicators

The circumstances of the following categories of persons are indicators for defining them as requiring additional diligence:

- Persons residing in and/or having funds sourced from countries identified by credible sources as having inadequate anti-money laundering standards or representing high-risk for crime and corruption.
- Persons engaged in types of business activities or sectors known to be susceptible to money laundering.
- *Politically Exposed Persons* (PEPs), referring to individuals holding or having held positions of public trust, such as government officials, senior executives of government corporations, politicians, important political party officials, etc., as well as their families and close associates.

Senior management approval

The banks' internal policies should indicate whether, for any one or more among these categories, senior management must approve entering into new relationships.

Relationships with *Politically Exposed Persons* may only be entered into with the approval of senior management.

C. Updating client files

- The private banker is responsible for updating the client file on a defined basis and/or when there are major changes. The private banker's supervisor or an independent control person will review relevant portions of client files on a regular basis to ensure consistency and completeness. The frequency of the reviews depends on the size and complexity of, and risk posed by, the relationship.
- With respect to clients classified under any category of persons mentioned in section B, the bank's internal policies will indicate whether the senior management must be involved in these reviews.
- Similarly, with respect to clients classified as set forth in 3.2, the bank's internal policies will indicate what management information must be provided to management and/or other control layers. The policies should also address the frequency of these information flows.
- The reviews of PEPs must require senior management's involvement.

D. Practices when identifying unusual or suspicious activities

Definition of unusual or suspicious activities

The bank will have a written policy on the identification of and follow-up on unusual or suspicious activities. This policy will include a definition of what is considered to be suspicious or unusual and give examples thereof. Unusual or suspicious activities may include:

- Account transactions or other activities which are not consistent with the due diligence file
- Cash transactions over a certain amount
- Pass-through / in-and-outtransactions.

Identification of unusual or suspicious activities

Unusual or suspicious activities can be identified through:

- Monitoring of transactions
- Client contacts (meetings, discussions, in-country visits, etc.)
- Third party information (e.g. newspapers, Reuters, Internet)
- Private bankers / internal knowledge of the client's environment (e.g. political situation in his/her country).

Follow-up on unusual or suspicious activities

The private banker, management, and/or the control function will carry out an analysis of the background of any unusual or suspicious activity. If there is no plausible explanation, a decision will be made involving the control function:

- To continue the business relationship with increased monitoring
- To cancel the business relationship
- To report the business relationship to the authorities

The report to the authorities is made by the control function and the senior management may need to be notified (e.g. senior compliance officer, CEO, chief auditor, general counsel). As required by local laws and regulations, the assets may be blocked and transactions may be subject to approval by the control function.

E. Monitoring

Monitoring program

A sufficient monitoring program must be in place. The primary responsibility for monitoring account activities lies with the private banker. The private banker will be familiar with significant transactions and increased activity in the account and will be especially aware of unusual or suspicious activities (see 4.1). The bank will decide to what extent fulfillment of these responsibilities will need to be supported through the use of automated systems or other means.

Ongoing monitoring

With respect to clients classified under any category of persons mentioned in 2, the bank's internal policies will indicate how the account activities will be subject to monitoring.

F. Control responsibilities

A written control policy will be in place, establishing standard control procedures to be undertaken by the various control layers (private banker, independent operations unit, compliance, and internal audit). The control policy will cover issues of timing, degree of control, areas to be controlled, responsibilities and follow-up, etc. An independent audit function (which may be internal to the bank) will test the programs contemplated by the control policy.

G. Reporting

There will be regular management reporting established on money laundering issues (e.g. number of reports to authorities, monitoring tools, changes in applicable laws and regulations, and the number and scope of training sessions provided to employees).

H. Education, training and information

The bank will establish a training program on the identification and prevention of money laundering for employees who have client contact and for compliance personnel. Regular training (e.g. annually) will also include how to identify and follow-up on unusual or suspicious activities. In addition, employees will be informed about any major changes in anti-money laundering laws and regulations.

All new employees will be provided with guidelines on the anti-money laundering procedures.

I. Record retention requirements

The bank will establish record retention requirements for all anti-money laundering related documents. The documents must be kept for a minimum of five years.

J. Exceptions and deviations

The bank will establish an exception and deviation procedure that requires risk assessment and approval by an independent unit.

K. Anti-money laundering organization

The bank will establish an adequately staffed and independent department responsible for the prevention of money laundering (e.g. compliance, independent control unit, legal).

Wolfsberg statement on the suppression of the financing of terrorism

The Wolfsberg Group of Financial Institutions (Wolfsberg Group) is committed to contributing to the fight against terrorism and is making the following statement to describe the role of financial institutions in preventing the flow of terrorist funds through the world's financial system.

This fight presents new challenges. Funds used in the financing of terrorism do not necessarily derive from criminal activity, which is a requisite element of most existing money laundering offences. Successful participation in this fight by the financial sector requires global cooperation by governments with the financial institutions to an unprecedented degree.

Role of Financial Institutions in the Fight against Terrorism

Financial institutions can assist governments and their agencies in the fight against terrorism. They can help this effort through prevention, detection, and information sharing. They should seek to prevent terrorist organizations from accessing their financial services, assist governments in their efforts to detect suspected terrorist financing, and promptly respond to governmental enquiries.

Rights of the Individual

The Wolfsberg Group is committed to participating in the fight against terrorism in a manner which is non-discriminatory and is respectful of the rights of individuals.

Know Your Customer

The Wolfsberg Group recognizes that adherence to existing Know Your Customer policies and procedures is important to the fight against terrorism. Specifically, the proper identification of customers by financial institutions can improve the efficacy of searches against lists of known or suspected terrorists issued by competent authorities having jurisdiction over the relevant financial institution (applicable lists).

In addition to the continued application of existing customer identification and acceptance and due diligence procedures, the Wolfsberg Group is committed to:

- Implementing procedures for consulting applicable lists and taking reasonable and practicable steps to determine whether a person involved in a prospective or existing business relationship appears on such a list.
- Reporting to relevant authorities matches from lists of known or suspected terrorists or terrorist organizations consistent with applicable laws and regulations regarding the disclosure of customer information.

- Exploring with governmental agencies ways of improving information exchange within and between jurisdictions.
- Exploring ways of improving the maintenance of customer information to facilitate the timely retrieval of such information.

High-Risk Sectors and Activities

The Wolfsberg Group is committed to applying enhanced and appropriate due diligence in relation to those of their customers engaged in sectors and activities identified by competent authorities as being widely used for the financing of terrorism, such as underground banking businesses or alternative remittance systems. This will include the adoption, to the extent not already in place, of specific policies and procedures on acceptance of business from customers engaged in such sectors or activities, and increased monitoring of activity of customers who meet the relevant acceptance criteria.

In particular, the Wolfsberg Group is committed to restricting their business relationships with remittance businesses, exchange houses, *casas de cambio*, *bureaux de change*, and money transfer agents to those which are subject to appropriate regulation aimed at preventing such activities and businesses from being used as a conduit to launder the proceeds of crime and/or finance terrorism.

The Wolfsberg Group recognizes that many jurisdictions are currently in the process of developing and implementing regulations with regard to these businesses, and that appropriate time needs to be given for these regulations to take effect.

Monitoring recognizes the difficulties inherent in identifying financial transactions linked to the financing of terrorism (many of which appear routine in relation to information known at the time). The Wolfsberg Group is committed to the continued application of existing monitoring procedures for identifying unusual or suspicious transactions. The Wolfsberg Group recognizes that while the motive for such transactions may be unclear, monitoring and then identifying and reporting unusual or suspicious transactions may assist government agencies by linking seemingly unrelated activity to the financing of terrorism.

In addition, the Wolfsberg Group is committed to:

- Exercising heightened scrutiny in respect of customers engaged in sectors identified by competent authorities as being widely used for the financing of terrorism.
- Monitoring account and transactional activity (to the extent meaningful information is available to financial institutions) against lists generated by competent authorities of known or suspected terrorists or terrorist organizations.
- Working with governments and agencies in order to recognize patterns and trends identified as related to the financing of terrorism.
- Considering the modification of existing monitoring procedures as necessary to assist in the identification of such patterns and trends.

Need for Enhanced Global Cooperation

The Wolfsberg Group is committed to co-operating with and assisting law enforcement and government agencies in their efforts to combat the financing of terrorism. The Wolfsberg Group has identified the following areas for discussion with governmental agencies, with a view to enhancing the contribution financial institutions are able to make:

- The provision of official lists of suspected terrorists and terrorist organizations on a globally coordinated basis by the relevant competent authority in each jurisdiction.
- The inclusion of appropriate details and information in official lists to assist financial institutions in efficient and timely searches of their customer bases. This information should ideally include (where known) in the case of individuals: date of birth, place of birth, and passport or identity card number; in the case of corporations: place of

incorporation or establishment, details of principals, to the extent possible, reason for inclusion on the list, and geographic information, such as the location, date, and time of the transaction.

- Providing prompt feedback to financial institutions on reports made following circulation of such official lists.
- The provision of meaningful information in relation to patterns, techniques, and mechanisms used in the financing of terrorism to assist with monitoring procedures.
- The provision of meaningful information about corporate and other types of vehicles used to facilitate terrorist financing.
- The development of guidelines on appropriate levels of heightened scrutiny in relation to sectors or activities identified by competent authorities as being widely used for terrorist financing.
- The development by governments and clearing agencies of uniform global formats for funds transfers that require information which may assist their efforts to prevent and detect the financing of terrorism.
- Ensuring that national legislation:

  1. Permits financial institutions to maintain information derived from official lists within their own databases and to share such information within their own groups.
  2. Affords financial institutions protection from civil liability for relying on such lists.
  3. Permits financial institutions to report unusual or suspicious transactions that may relate to terrorism to the relevant authorities without breaching any duty of customer confidentiality or privacy legislation.
  4. Permits the prompt exchange of information between governmental agencies of different nation states.

The Wolfsberg Group supports the FATF Special Recommendations on Terrorist Financing as measures conducive to the suppression of the financing of terrorism.

Other initiatives include:

> ➤ Law enforcement of various countries issued control lists of names of individuals and companies identified as having possible terrorist links.
> ➤ The United States Congress passed the Patriot Act of 2001 (Title III), the international money laundering abatement and anti-terrorist financing Act of 2001
> ➤ Sec. 314 of the Patriot Act now required the United States Treasury Department to adopt regulations encouraging information sharing among law enforcement agencies, regulators, and financial institutions, after providing notice to Treasury, to share information with each other regarding suspected terrorist or money launderers.
> ➤ The Office of Foreign Assets Control (OFAC)[10] issued an unprecedented number of updates adding new names to the US sanctions list of entities and individuals linked to terrorism.
> ➤ The New York Clearing House issued guidelines for best practices in correspondent banking.

---

[10] The Office of Foreign Assets Control ("OFAC") is a small and powerful agency of the U.S. Treasury Department. It promulgates, interprets, and administers Treasury sanctions programs; it has several divisions responsible for compliance, legal issues, licensing, and penalties.

Examples of anti-money laundering laws:

Many countries have passed, or are in the process of passing, anti-money laundering laws and regulations. We will look at the United States of America laws, the European Union anti-money laundering directive, the Egyptian anti-money laundering law, and the Saudi Arabian anti-money laundering law in addition to other Arabian countries' initiatives.

The United States laws

A. Anunzio Wylie law:

Anunzio Wylie law gives the United States regulators the ability to grant and take away licenses. It affects all banks chartered and licensed under the United States law with extraterritorial effect. A United States bank that knowingly aids and abets in the process and is convicted for money laundering or criminal violations of the Bank Secrecy Act provides authority to United States bank regulators to revoke the bank's charter or license and its Federal Deposit Insurance Corporation (FDIC) insurance (United States banks insurance for depositors when a bank files for bankruptcy) or require the bank to operate under a conservator. In addition, bank employees may face suspension or prohibition from further participation in any manner with the affairs of any banking institution. Under this law, if a bank pleads guilty or is convicted of money laundering, it must appear at a predetermination hearing before its primary regulator. Regulators will take into account a number of factors including:

1. The extent to which the institution's directors or senior management knew or were involved in criminal activity.
2. Whether the institution had policies and procedures designed to prevent the occurrence of a money laundering offence.
3. The extent to which the institution has cooperated with law enforcement officials in the investigation of the money laundering offences of which it was found guilty.
4. The extent to which the institution had instituted additional internal controls since the commission of the offence to prevent the occurrence of future money laundering offences.
5. The effect of the closing of the institution on the local community.
6. The answers to the above questions will dictate possible regulatory sanctions and enforcement actions. Less draconian measures include Memorandums of Understanding or Cease and Desist Orders, which will require the financial institutions to correct deficiencies.

Definition of knowledge under United States law

Knowledge is a key element of an offence under the United States anti-money laundering criminal statutes. The definition of knowing under United States laws includes:

➢ Actual knowledge
➢ Purposeful or deliberate ignorance or indifference or conscious avoidance
➢ Willful blindness
➢ Collective knowledge of information regarding the source and nature of proceeds

To illustrate, a bank officer who conducts a financial transaction without knowing that the proceeds involved are the revenues from drugs sales can still be guilty of money laundering if it can be proven that he or she knew the money was derived from some type of criminal activity. Similarly, an employee who engages in a financial transaction of more than a central bank reporting limit (10,000 dollars in the United States for an example) with a customer knowing that the funds involved come from drug sales commits the crime of money laundering. In both cases, the employee, the bank, and the customers conducting the transactions could face felony money laundering charges and substantial fines.

Under the purposeful indifference or deliberate ignorance doctrine, bankers must be proactive in identifying suspicious activities. For example, it is not enough that a customer tells the banker that a business or a transaction is legitimate. The banker has the obligation to conduct further due diligence.

Under the willful blindness doctrine, if a person deliberately avoids or ignores information which could have led to the discovery of unlawful activity because he or she wants to remain ignorant of the true nature of the activity, he or she could be held responsible for whatever knowledge an investigation would have revealed. A court would find that a defendant had criminal knowledge if the defendant is found to have consciously and/or deliberately avoided knowledge of facts, which would have disclosed criminal activity.

Under the collective knowledge doctrine, a bank is treated as if it possesses all the knowledge of all individuals (directors, officers, and employees). Governments may be able to prove a business entity's knowledge by offering evidence of the aggregate knowledge of the corporation's individual employees. This makes it crucial for banks to communicate effectively, both across and within functional areas.

The leading collective knowledge case involved a former United States bank called Bank of New England. The bank was convicted of failing to file a currency transaction report (a report required under United States laws for transactions exceeding 10,000 US dollars based on the aggregate knowledge of its employees (i.e., certain employees knew that cash transactions exceeded a central bank reporting limit, while others knew of the currency transaction report filing requirements) and finally, the bank's flagrant indifference to the reporting requirements. This led to the bank being convicted of criminal Bank Secrecy Act violations while individual employees were acquitted.

B. Sections 1956 and 1957 of the money laundering criminal statutes

This law contains several provisions that extend its prohibitions and powerful sanctions into foreign countries. The extraterritorial jurisdiction of the principal United States money laundering law can apply to a financial transaction that occurs in whole or part in the United States if the funds involved were derived from purely foreign crimes that include drug trafficking, extortion, fraud against a foreign bank, kidnapping, robbery, or destruction of property by explosion or fire. Below are examples of some areas where this concept may be applied:

1. A financial transaction that occurs in whole or part in the United States if the funds involved were derived from purely foreign crimes that include drug trafficking, extortion, fraud against a foreign bank, kidnapping, robbery, destruction of property, and bribery of a public official.
2. A funds transfer through a United States bank, or telephone calls or faxes to the United States in furtherance of the transaction could also be considered conduct occurring in part in the United States.
3. International transportation or transmissions from or to the United States of illicit proceeds to promote or carry on a specified unlawful activity or with knowledge that the funds are from some form of unlawful activity.

C. The United States Patriot Act

Even before the events of September 11, efforts by the United States government to expand the reach of anti-money laundering laws were a high priority for regulators, legislators, and law enforcement. Money laundering legislation had been introduced in both the United States House and Senate, and the United States Securities and Exchange Commission was about to begin its anti-money laundering compliance sweep at broker dealers.

The terrorist events of September 11 catapulted these efforts to the top of the agenda. The United States administration and Congress quickly agreed that cracking down on international money laundering and terrorist financing would be a key element to the war against terrorism. One notable result is the prompt enactment of the United States of America Patriot Act of 2001 that the United States president signed into law in October 2001. This Act arguably represents the most significant anti-money laundering legislation for financial institutions since the enactment of the Bank Secrecy Act in 1970. Many of the new requirements explicitly need implementing regulation, and others need regulations to provide clarification and specificity. These requirements are complex and in most cases will require substantial effort to implement.

The Patriot Act is a significant and sweeping money laundering legislation. It applies anti-money laundering provisions to all terrorist assets, including legally obtained funds, if intended for use in planning, committing, or concealing a terrorist act. The act mandates that all financial institutions have anti-money laundering programs. It also prohibits United States financial institutions from providing correspondent banking services to foreign shell banks, directly or indirectly. The Act targets foreign jurisdictions with legal and regulatory structures that may create a high-risk of money laundering mandating new enhanced due diligence procedures, particularly for private banking and correspondent banking relationships.In addition, the Act gives the United States government the authority to seize assets held in a foreign bank.

The Act extended the extraterritorial reach of the United States government. Section 317 of the Act provides the United States district courts under certain circumstances with long arm jurisdiction over, among others, foreign financial institutions formed under the laws of a foreign country, if, among other things, the foreign financial institution maintains a bank account at a financial institution in the United States.

Section 319 of the Act includes provision broadening the ability of the government to seize and forfeit assets held in a foreign bank, if the foreign bank has an interbank account in the United States. This section also provides that the Secretary of the Treasury or the Attorney General may issue a summons or subpoena to any foreign bank that maintains a correspondent account in the United States and request records related to such an account, including records maintained outside the United States relating to the deposit of funds into the foreign bank. (Foreign banks are required to provide the name of an agent for service of process on the certifications they provided to their United States correspondent banks).

Upon receipt of notice from the Secretary or the Attorney General, a United States bank that maintains a correspondent account has ten business days to terminate a correspondent relationship with a foreign bank. Such a notification will only be made after the Treasury and Justice Departments consult with each other, and a determination is made that the foreign bank has failed to comply with a summons or a subpoena issued under this section of the Act.

Penalties under United States laws

Financial institutions that are convicted or plead guilty to an indictment of money laundering are subject to corporate sentencing guidelines including a maximum fine of 290 million dollars and a possible forfeiture of assets. Individuals may be subject to a maximum prison term of twenty years and a fine of half a million dollars or double the value of the money laundered.

Corporate criminal liability

This is a unique American concept that states a corporation is liable for the acts of its employees. That is a business entity may be convicted based on crimes of any employee if its employee's culpable conduct was committed:

➤ Within the scope of their actual or apparent authority, means in connection with the performance of some job-related function

➤ With the intent, in part, to benefit the business entity (benefit is broadly defined: monetary gain, service, public relations)

Single employees who engage in criminal conduct may cause the entire corporation to be subjected to criminal sanctions even if the employee acts against corporate policy or even if the employee acts against expressed company instructions.

The corporation can be convicted even if the employee is not criminally charged or is acquitted. The government may forfeit all of the property involved in the money laundering transactions including accounts, collateral, or mortgaged property. New York State criminal statutes, for instance, criminalize the proceeds of any crime under New York law or any crime conducted in another jurisdiction, e.g., another state of foreign country, that would be a crime under New York law.

The European Union (EU) anti-money laundering directive

The European Union issued a Council Directive in June 1991 on prevention of the use of the financial system for the purpose of money laundering. The directive, which has eighteen articles, requires member states to ensure money laundering is prohibited. It requires member states to ensure credit and financial institutions keep the following for use as evidence in any investigation into money laundering:

➤ In case of identification, a copy or the references of the evidence required, for a period of at least five years after the relationship with their customer has ended,

➤ In case of transactions, the supporting evidence and records, consisting of the original documents or copies admissible in court proceedings under the applicable national legislation for a period of at least five years following execution of the transactions.

The directive further requires member states to:

➢ Ensure that credit and financial institutions examine, with special attention, any transaction they regard as particularly likely, by its nature, to be related to money laundering.

➢ Ensure that credit and financial institutions and their directors and employees cooperate fully with the authorities responsible for combating money laundering by informing those authorities, on their own initiative, of any fact that might be an indication of money laundering and by furnishing those authorities, at their request, with all necessary information, in accordance with the procedures established by the applicable legislation.

➢ Ensure that credit and financial institutions refrain from carrying out transactions which they know or suspect to be related to money laundering until they have apprised the authorities.

➢ Not to disclose to the customer concerned or to other third persons that information has been transmitted to the authorities.

➢ Ensure that if, in the course of inspections carried out in credit or financial institutions by the competent authorities, or in any other way, those authorities discover facts that could constitute evidence of money laundering, they inform the authorities responsible for combating money laundering.

➢ Ensure that credit and financial institutions establish adequate procedures of internal control and communication in order to forestall and prevent operations related to money laundering and take appropriate measures so that their employees are aware of the provisions contained in this directive.

➢ Ensure that the provisions of this directive are extended, in whole or in part, to professions and to categories of undertakings that engage in activities that are particularly likely to be used for money laundering purposes.

➢ Establish a contact committee to:

(a) Facilitate harmonized implementation of this directive through regular consultation on any practical problems arising from its application and on which exchanges of view are deemed useful

(b) Facilitate consultation between the member states on the more stringent or additional conditions and obligations which they may lay down at national level

(c) Advise the Commission, if necessary, on any supplements or amendments to be made to the directive or on any adjustments deemed necessary

(d) Examine whether a profession or a category of undertaking should be included in the scope of the directive where it has been established that such profession or category of undertaking has been used in a member state for money laundering.

In November of 2001, the European Union Council of Ministers approved revisions to the European Union's anti-money laundering directive broadening the definition of targeted criminal activity from drug offence proceeds (as per original directive), to include proceeds from all serious crimes. The directive imposes anti-money laundering obligations on gatekeepers. The modifications require a broad range of professionals (including independent legal professionals, accountants, auditors, and notaries) to abide by anti-money laundering regulations within eighteen months of the date of adoption.

The Egyptian anti-money laundering law

In May 2002, Egypt enacted Law No. 80-2002 for combating money laundering. The law criminalizes the laundering of proceeds from various crimes, including narcotics, terrorism, fraud, and organized crime. The law addresses customer identification, record keeping, and establishes the framework for the Money Laundering Combating Unit (MLCU) to function as a financial investigation unit within the Central Bank of Egypt.

Law no. 78-2003 came into effect in June 2003. It enhanced the scope of Law no. 80-2002 by expanding the predicate offences and removing a previous loophole that appeared to grant broad exemptions from imprisonment. Prime Minister Decree

No. 951-2003 detailed the Executive Regulations for Law no. 80-2002 and came into effect in June 2003. The Regulations further detailed anti-money laundering obligations for financial institutions, including banks, *bureaux de change*, money remittance, securities, and insurance. The regulations also detailed the requirement for suspicious activity reporting, customer identification procedures, the functions of the MLCU, supervision of entities for compliance with the obligations, and international cooperation.

Some specific requirements of the law

> The law prohibits laundering of funds that are the proceeds of the crimes of planting, manufacturing, and smuggling narcotics or psychotropic substances, or trafficking therein, the crimes of hijacking means of transport and detaining of individuals, the crimes in which terrorism or the financing thereof falls among its purposes or means of perpetration, the crimes of unlicensed importation, trading and manufacturing of weaponry, ammunition, and explosives, the crimes of money theft and usurpation, debauchery and prostitution, any crimes against antiquities, environmental crimes related to dangerous wastes and materials, and organized crimes.

> An independent unit with a special nature shall be established at the Central Bank of Egypt to combat money laundering, wherein the concerned entities shall be represented.

> The entities assigned by laws and regulations to supervise financial institutions shall be obliged to establish and provide adequate means for verifying that the said institutions comply with the systems and rules legally established for combating money laundering, including reporting of transactions suspected of involving money laundering.

> Financial institutions are obliged to report to the unit any suspicious financial transactions that may involve money laundering, and to establish systems that ensure the obtaining of information on the identification and legal status of their customers and the beneficial owners, whether natural or legal persons, through official or acceptable customary verification

means, and to register the information concerning such identification. Financial institutions are prohibited from opening accounts or accepting deposits, funds or trusts of anonymous origin, or under false or fictitious names.

➤ Financial institutions are obliged to keep records and documents for local and international financial transactions containing sufficient information for identifying such transactions; and they should maintain these records and documents and the registers for customers and beneficiaries' information for a period of no less than five years from the date the transaction is finalized with the financial institution, or from the date of closing the account, as the case may be.

➤ No criminal liability action shall be brought against any person who, in good faith, reports any suspicious financial transactions.

➤ It shall be prohibited to disclose to the customer, the beneficiary, or any authorities other than those responsible for enforcing the provisions of this law, any of the procedures relating to reporting, investigation, and examination regarding any financial transaction suspected of involving money laundering or any related information.

➤ Travelers shall still be entitled to carry foreign currency into or out of the country under the law, provided that upon arrival, they declare amounts exceeding twenty thousand US dollars, or their equivalent, on the form prepared by the unit, and subject to its rules.

➤ Without prejudice to any severer sanctions stipulated under the penal code or any other laws, the crimes stated in the following provisions shall be penalized by the sanctions provided hereunder.

    a. Any person who commits or attempts to commit a money laundering crime under this law shall be imprisoned for a period not exceeding seven years, and fined a sum twice the amount of money subject of the crime. In all cases, the seized funds shall be confiscated or an additional fine equivalent to the value of these funds shall be imposed if such funds cannot be seized, or have been disposed to others in good faith.

b. A person who violates this law shall be penalized by imprisonment and fined an amount not less than five thousand Egyptian pounds and not more than twenty thousand Egyptian pounds, or either.

c. In case the crime is committed by a legal entity, the natural person responsible for actual management of the violating entity shall be penalized by the same sanctions stipulated for the acts in violation of the provisions of this law if it is established that such person had known about the crime, and the crime was committed as a result of the violation of this person's duties.

➤ Egyptian judicial authorities shall cooperate with its foreign counterparts in the field of money laundering crimes, with respect to judicial assistance, extradition of accused and convicted persons and the transfer of any related things, in accordance with the rules under bilateral or multilateral treaties to which Egypt is a party, or on the basis of the reciprocity principle.

➤ The authorities referred to in this law may, in particular, request the adoption of legal measures necessary to trace, seize, or freeze the funds or proceeds involved in money laundering crimes without prejudice to the rights of good faith of third parties.

➤ Subject to the bilateral or multilateral treaties to which Egypt is a party, the competent Egyptian judicial authorities may order the enforcement of final criminal judgments rendered by competent foreign judicial authorities, concerning the confiscation of the proceeds and revenue of money laundering. Bilateral or multilateral treaties may be concluded to regulate the disposal of funds confiscated by final judgments regarding money-laundering crimes rendered by Egyptian or foreign judicial authorities, and such treaties shall include rules for distributing the said funds among the parties concerned in accordance with the provisions stipulated therein.

Saudi Arabia anti-money laundering law

Saudi Arabia is a growing financial center in the Gulf region of the Middle East. There is little money laundering in Saudi Arabia related to narcotics trafficking and other traditional predicate offences. However, Saudi Arabia has increased its attention on money laundering activity following the September 11 terrorist attacks and has made contributions in the war on terrorist financing.

In Saudi Arabia, money laundering is subject to prosecution based on *Sharia* (Islamic) law, the Banking Control Law, and Saudi Arabian labor law. Jurisdiction over money laundering offences lies in the *Sharia* courts. Saudi Arabia has had a small number of prosecutions for money laundering that originated from the filing of suspicious transaction reports.

Saudi law prohibits non-resident individuals or corporations from opening bank accounts in Saudi Arabia without the specific authorization of the Saudi Arabian Monetary Authority (SAMA). SAMA guidelines correspond to the Financial Action Task Force (FATF) Forty Recommendations and the Nine Special Recommendations on terrorists financing, and specifically require banks to enforce Know Your Customer rules, maintain records of suspicious transactions, and inform SAMA of suspicious transactions. SAMA has been active in providing anti-money laundering training to Saudi financial institutions. The government has established an anti-money laundering unit in SAMA and has required Saudi banks to have anti-money laundering units and staff to work with SAMA and law enforcement authorities. The government has also recently created a Financial Intelligence Unit (FIU) in the Security and Drug Control Department of the Ministry of the Interior. The new FIU is tasked with handling money-laundering cases and coordinating its activities with SAMA and appropriate law enforcement agencies.

Saudi Arabia has signed the International Convention for the Suppression and Financing of Terrorism based on United Nations Security Council Resolution number 1373. The government signed a multilateral agreement under the auspices of the Arab League to fight terrorism. Saudi Arabia also invited the FATF to carry out a mutual evaluation in September 2003 against the FATF Forty Recommendations and the Special Eight Recommendations on terrorist financing.

Saudi Arabia has established a High Commission for oversight of all charities. Charities in Saudi Arabia must be licensed, registered, audited, and supervised. Contributions to charities are usually *Zakat*, which is an Islamic religious duty with specified humanitarian purposes. New guidelines, regulations, and financial control mechanisms have been implemented to help counteract the misuse of charitable donations.

Saudi Arabia has passed specific anti-money laundering and anti-terrorist financing laws and has moved very rapidly to enforce the new regulations and guidelines established to counteract money laundering and terrorists financing.

The twenty-nine articles law stipulates jail terms of up to fifteen years and a fine of 1.86 million dollars for money laundering through charities or organized gangs. The anti-money laundering law makes terrorism financing or terror organizations punishable offences. Other money laundering offenders will face a maximum of ten years in jail and a fine of 1.3 million dollars, according to the legislation.

The law requires financial institutions to keep records of transactions for a minimum of ten years and adopt precautionary measures to uncover and foil money laundering operations. It also requires financial institutions to create financial intelligence units to prepare reports on suspicious transactions to help minimize and detect such illegal operations. The law also prohibits financial institutions from opening anonymous number or coded accounts. It also allows exchange of information and judicial action against money laundering operations with countries with which the Kingdom maintains official agreements.

Other Arabian Countries

Bahrain: Bahrain is vulnerable to money laundering because it is a regional financial and offshore center. The most common sources of illegal proceeds in Bahrain include narcotics trafficking, fraud, and evasion of international sanctions. Bahrain recently passed legislation that criminalizes money laundering and obligates financial institutions to report suspicious transactions greater than 26,000 US dollars to the Bahrain Monetary Authority. Bahrain is a party to the 1988 United Nations Drug Convention.

Jordan: Jordan is not a regional financial center, and the government of Jordan regulates foreign exchange transactions. Jordan has not yet criminalized any form of money laundering. Jordanian law enforcement officials report that some financial institutions cooperate with prosecutors' requests for information related to drug trafficking cases. Central bank has instructed financial institutions to look out for customers engaging in dubious transfers and be particularly careful when handling foreign currency transactions. Jordan is a party to the 1988 United Nation Drug Convention.

Lebanon: The current legal, supervisory, and regulatory systems of Lebanon create significant opportunities for the laundering and protection of the proceeds of crime. Weaknesses in these systems allow criminals to evade effective investigation and punishment. Laundering in Lebanon takes place through the layering of transactions in banks and through the purchase of property and businesses. Lebanon's commitment to bank secrecy and the absence of certain key supervisory and enforcement mechanisms aimed at preventing and detecting money-laundering activities increase the possibility that transactions involving Lebanese entities and accounts will be used for illegal purposes. An anti-narcotics law that came into effect in 1998 criminalized drug-related money laundering. The Lebanese cabinet approved a draft law in December 2000. The draft law broadens the definition of money laundering to include proceeds obtained from organized crime, illegal arms trafficking, embezzlement of public funds, and counterfeiting of currencies and official documents.

The United Arab Emirates (UAE): The country's position as a major financial and trading center in the Gulf region of the Middle East makes it vulnerable to money laundering. Evidence from international financial crimes investigations shows money-laundering connections to the UAE. There are no foreign exchange controls, no corporate or income taxes, and the UAE has free trade zones. The UAE is also a regional gold center, which is often manipulated by money launderers around the world via trade or as part of alternative remittance systems such as the *Hawala* system. In an effort to address these vulnerabilities, the central bank recently mandated capital reserve requirements of over thirteen million US dollars for prospective currency dealers and money-exchange houses. The net effect of this move will be to ensure that a larger percentage of the remittance business flows through the better-regulated banking system. Existing UAE laws on narcotics trafficking are broad and extremely strict; those involved in handling drug money in any way may be subject to the death penalty.

A money-laundering law has recently been passed which includes criminal penalties. The central bank has issued new regulations for all banks, moneychangers, and finance companies in an effort to check money laundering. They require the reporting of all cash transactions exceeding 54,500 US dollars and all suspicious transactions to the central bank. The central bank is able to freeze suspect funds, make appropriate inquiries, and coordinate with law enforcement officials. The UAE has recently established a unit within the central bank to act as a Financial Intelligence Unit (FIU), charged with examining suspicious activity reporting and handling all requests from law enforcement and judicial authorities. The UAE is a party to the 1988 United Nation Drug Convention.

Issues of concern such as the misuse of the international gold trade and the use of *Hawala* to laundered funds are not unique to the UAE, and these forms of alternate remittance systems are extremely difficult to identify and combat.

How Is Money Laundered?

Money is laundered in three phases: placement, layering, and integration.

The placement phase

The first process, placement, involves the physical entry of bulk cash into the financial system. It is important to point out that cash does not have a trail. Most other forms of payment, such as checks, wires, and credit cards, show a link between the payee and the payor. This linking is undesirable to those who are involved in illegal activity since it may help law enforcement track and then seize funds derived from illicit activity.

For example, drugs are often purchased in the streets with cash. The money launderer must transform all of the cash in order to pay suppliers and make use of the profits. Cash can then:

1. Get deposited into the banking system (through *smurfing*, which is the conversion of cash to monetary instruments);
2. Be converted into monetary instrument (i.e. cashier's checks, money orders, and travelers check) for ease of transport around the world; or
3. Be used in the retail industry to purchase items such as cars, boats, planes, antiques, and artwork.

Both traditional financial institutions, such as banks and brokerage houses, and non-traditional financial institutions, such as currency exchanges, *casas de cambio*, casinos, and check cashing business, can be used during this phase. Let's illustrate the simplest and least sophisticated methods:

In one day in the United States of America capital, Washington, District of Columbia, for example, twenty-four million US dollars is sold in illicit drugs. If we assume that the twenty-four million US dollars is collected in twenty US dollars denominations, it would approximately weigh 2,600 pounds.

Placement of cash and bearer instruments into the financial system is known as *smurfing*—that is, having people deposit random amounts less than a central bank reporting limit into variously named accounts at many different banks. They will also buy monetary instruments from various financial institutions to circumvent a central bank's thresholds for transaction reporting. A middleman can then ship the instruments for deposit elsewhere. Smurfs are now engaging in structuring cash deposits as part of the Black Market Peso Exchange[11].

The Bank Secrecy Act (BSA), a United States law, requires financial institutions located in the United States and its possessions and territories to maintain records and report certain transactions to the United States government. BSA regulations that prevent and detect laundering during placement include currency reporting and record keeping rules, such as:

- Currency Transaction Report over cash transactions of 10,000 US dollars or higher,
- Currency Monetary Instruments Reports, and
- 3,000 US dollars recording requirement for monetary instruments

Placement evolved into structuring to avoid the threshold reporting of transactions of central banks reporting limits.

---

[11] The Black Market Peso Exchange system is a trade-based system that depends on commercial traffic between the United.States and Colombia to launder profits from the sale of illegal drugs in the United States.

Structuring occurs when a customer breaks down transactions below certain currency amounts for the purpose of evading a reporting requirement (in the United States, 10,000 dollars) or avoiding detection. In many countries, structuring is itself a crime, even if the funds are legitimately derived, and structuring, whenever it occurs, is a sign of possible money laundering. Structuring carries monetary fines for individuals and for corporations.

These measures have been so effective in frustrating the money launderer that it is estimated that 80 percent of the funds generated by narcotics trafficking in the United States are now bulk smuggled out of the country. For example, someone might smuggle cash to Mexico, deposit it in a Mexican Bank, purchase a bank draft, and mail or carry it back into the United States for deposit or to cash it in a United States bank. This has major implications for financial institutions, since financial institutions outside the United States in countries with weak regulatory controls are now targeted for placement, while United States financial institutions are now seeing more money laundering during the layering or integration stages of the process where it is more difficult to detect.

Examples of the placement phase:

> Cash currency smuggled out in passenger luggage, bulk container shipments, or other means of smuggling
> Smurfing
> Cash deposits placed in consumer accounts opened by money brokers for a cartel as part of the Black Market for Peso Exchange
> Making deposits to credit card accounts through the Automated Teller Machine (ATM), followed by withdrawals after short periods of time, particularly when the withdrawals are made in another country

The layering phase:

In the middle 1990s, money laundering took on increasingly sophisticated and complex method. Layering, the second phase of multiple financial transactions designed to break an audit trail, disguises the origin of the funds and provides anonymity.

Unusual signs of layering include a request by a client to purchase a product where the source of funds to purchase the product is inconsistent with the customer's financial standing or is a third party check. Or a customer who does not wish to know about the performance of an investment but is concerned only about the early cancellation provisions of a particular product.

To demonstrate how layering takes place, let's look at three products: annuity, back-to-back loans, and trade transactions:

Annuity:

A particular area where the life insurance industry is vulnerable is the single premium product (annuity). This is attractive to launderers because they can purchase the product and come back to the financial institution that sold it to them within the free look period (ten to thirty days) and cash in the product for a full refund with no penalty. They will walk out with a check drawn on that financial institution. So the launderer can place dirty funds in Bank A, wire the funds to Bank B to purchase an annuity, cash out an annuity, and go to Bank C with a cashier's check from Bank B that looks perfectly legitimate.

Back-to-Back loans:

Back-to-Back loans become risky when the customer asks for a loan against collateral that the bank is holding (perhaps a certificate of deposit or a time deposit), and the appropriate due diligence has not been done upfront when the original investment was made. While the bank may have collateral to cover its credit risk, it must ascertain that the source of funds of that collateral is legitimate, so in the event the due diligence was not done upfront when the time deposit was established, it should be done at this juncture. If illegitimate funds are involved, the funds are subject to forfeiture.

Trade transactions:

Trade transactions involving letters of credit are a good vehicle to launder money since goods may be undervalued or overvalued, or the quantity or quality of the goods that actually moves with a transaction may be very different than the value stated on the letter of credit.

Other examples of the layering phase:

➤ Separation of illegal proceeds from their source through layers of complex financial transactions
➤ Wire transfers
➤ Multiple credit refunds or building a large credit balance on a credit or charge card with a subsequent request to close the account, resulting in an issued refund check

The integration phase:

Integration, the third phase, involves placing the proceeds back into the economy in such a way that they reenter the financial system as apparently legitimate funds.

At this stage of the process, money laundering is very difficult to detect. The key question is whether there is a legitimate source of funds and income. Unusual activity includes requests by customers for investment management services (either foreign currency or securities) where the source of funds is inconsistent with the customer's apparent standing, large or unusual settlements of securities in cash form, and buying and selling a security with no discernible purpose.

To illustrate, bank credit or charge cards can be used as an integration tool where funds can be repatriated through a debit or credit or charge card issued by an offshore bank without leaving a financial trail. The banks assure their clients the card account information is protected by the same rules that protect other account information.

An offshore company can also settle bills incurred at home offshore through their deposit account or even more discreetly.

In the United States, a landmark court ruling has given the Internal Revenue Service (IRS) the authority to seek information on Unites States citizens who may be laundering money or evading taxes through the use of offshore credit, charge, and debit cards. A United States judge authorized the IRS to issue John Doe summonses on American Express and MasterCard to determine the correct federal tax liabilities of taxpayers who have signatory authority over credit, charge, or debit cards issued by or through banks in Antigua, Bahamas, and the Cayman Islands.

Examples of the integration phase:

➢ Investments (stocks and bonds, mutual funds, and real estate)
➢ Use of bank credit, charge, and debit cards
➢ Capital construction projects

Obviously, the source of funding of the above examples is dirty money.

Recent money laundering trends:

FATF has also recently identified the following money laundering trends:

➢ Wire transfer and shell company activity
➢ Computer intrusion
➢ Money transmitters
➢ Identity theft
➢ Terrorist financing
➢ Alternative money remittance systems
➢ Black Market Peso Exchange System
➢ *Hawala* (underground banking) system (unlicensed transfers of funds and/or lack of controls on such transfers)

➢ Lawyers, notaries, accountants, and other non-financial professionals
➢ Market for gold and other precious metals
➢ Use of travelers checks to disguise identities
➢ Prepaid telephone cards as a cover for money laundering

Examples of frequent suspicious activity that illustrate the above trends are:

1. Wire and shell activity: many suspicious activity reports reference suspicious wire transfer activity involving possible shell entities as parties to the wire transfer activity. This activity has often involved the so-called unsubstantiated entities (companies that cannot be found through the internet or other research).

2. Suspicious activity reports related to money transmitters typically involve attempts to disperse transactions and circumvent record keeping dollar amount thresholds (structuring).

3. Alternate remittance systems operating outside the framework of supervision and regulation, and therefore provide anonymity and secrecy for all sorts of financial transactions. *Hawalas* are a type of alternative remittance system that operates in Asia.

4. Gold is known to play a significant role in international money laundering because it is a nearly universal commodity for international commerce.

What can financial institutions do to protect themselves?

Financial institutions can protect themselves by establishing a meaningful anti-money laundering and combating terrorists financing compliance program that contains the following measures:

Creation of an anti-money laundering and anti-terrorists financing unit:

The first measure is the creation of an anti-money laundering and combating terrorists financing unit with designated compliance officers responsible for coordinating and monitoring day-to-day compliance.

Financial institutions must establish an independent and dedicated anti-money laundering and combating terrorists financing control unit to detect and combat money laundering and terrorist financing activities. The unit should be responsible for reviewing, studying, and investigating any suspected money laundering and terrorist financing activities. The unit should participate in developing and implementing money laundering and terrorist financing programs, plans, procedures, and employees training. The designated compliance officers should:

➤ Be knowledgeable with the ways any of the financial institution's products and services may be abused by money launderers and terrorists

➤ Assist the financial institution in developing effective anti-money laundering and anti-terrorists financing enhanced due diligence programs including training.

➤ Assist the financial institution in assessing the vulnerability to money laundering of the products under development in order to establish appropriate controls before product is rolled out.

➤ Assist financial institution in evaluating whether questionable activity is suspicious under the applicable laws.

➤ Be familiar with anti-money laundering and anti-terrorist financing materials and documents issued by local authorities, international organizations such as FATF and other local or international bodies.

Developing a Know Your Customer (KYC) program:

Financial institutions should develop a Know Your Customer program that provides for:

a. Identification of clients at account opening or at inception of a business relationship and

b. Collection and verification of additional information commensurate with the client's risk assessment.

Know Your Customer has long been an axiom of effecting marketing of financial products and services and a requisite for prudent banking. In addition to protecting the institution, banks can better serve their customers if they understand their banking needs through enhanced due diligence programs.

The objectives of the KYC and enhanced due diligence program should be to:

➤ Protect the reputation of the organization
➤ Protect the privacy of the organization's customers

> Protect the organization from becoming a victim of illegal activities
> Promote ethical and professional standards within the financial sector
> Facilitate the identification of suspicious or illicit activities
> Facilitate compliance with applicable laws and adherence to sound practices

For a KYC program to work effectively, the following presumptions should be made:

> The majority of customers of an organization do not pose a risk of illicit activity at or through the organization.
> The majority of customers who do not pose a risk will not require increased scrutiny (the reporting of suspicious activity should still be required under existing regulations).
> Identification of categories of customers whose banking activities are routine and usual will assist in determining the majority of customers that will not require increased scrutiny.

If we consider the above facts, statistically, only a small percentage of a financial institution's customers truly present a threat of money laundering and terrorists financing. Therefore, enhanced due diligence efforts need to be focused on those entities and individuals, that through risk assessment, are deemed to warrant upfront enhanced due diligence and enhanced scrutiny of their transactions on an ongoing basis. These efforts must be focused.

Section 312 of the United States Patriot Act, e.g., establishes by regulation special measures for enhanced due diligence for private banking and correspondent accounts. There are also additional measures for such accounts held by foreign financial institutions operating under offshore licenses or licenses from jurisdictions designated as non-cooperative (FATF NCCTs)[12], or

---

[12] A FATF published list to identify non-cooperative countries and territories (NCCTs) in the fight against money laundering. Specifically, these are countries with critical weaknesses in anti-money laundering systems that serve as obstacles to international cooperation in this area.

from jurisdictions that the United States Treasury has identified as warranting special measures due to money laundering and terrorists financing concerns.

Elements of KYC programs:

An effective KYC program should be based on the following elements:

a. Customer identification

Know Your Customer programs should be designed to determine the true identity of all clients who establish a relationship with the financial institution, open accounts, or conduct significant transactions with the institution. It should also cater for obtaining and documenting any additional customer information, commensurate with the assessment of the money laundering risk posed by the clients' expected use of products and services. It should be designed to protect the financial institution from the risks of conducting business with individuals or entities whose identity cannot be established, refuse to provide required information, or who have provided inconsistent information.

Financial institutions should have customer identification policies to obtain identifying information to determine the identity of their customers. Special name accounts (numbered or coded accounts) must not be permitted. Furthermore, the authority of persons doing financial transactions on behalf of others must also be established.

b. Customer and transaction profiling

Financial institutions should profile their clients and the transactional activity conducted by them and must use this information to evaluate the appropriateness and reasonableness of the client's transaction activity. Customer profile consists of customer identification (as explained above, financial institutions must always determine the true identity of all clients who establish relationships, open accounts, and/or conduct significant transactions), basic background information about the client, and the client's source of funds.

The source of funds and transaction monitoring explanations should consider the client's expected transaction trends, the source of wealth, and the clients' net income. The source of funds refers to the origin of, and the means of remittance for, funds sent to the bank and accepted for the initial account opening and subsequent significant incoming funds. Examples include: sale of a private business or property, liquidation of a financial investment, and transfer of an account relationship from another financial institution.

Source of wealth, on the other hand, refers to a description of the economic activities that have generated the customer's net worth. The identified source of wealth should be sufficient to account for the size of the relationship with the customer. Source of wealth information would normally be business ownership. The client's relationship with the business must be established including the nature of the business, location and geographic trade areas, names of partners (if any), and the nature of their involvement in the business. Sources of wealth may also be inheritance, wealth obtained from being a top executive, or a past profession, or investments.

Transaction profiles must also be prepared for every client. The transaction profile represents the client's anticipated usage of the financial institution's products and services. It should at least show the average number of transactions per month, their ranges, values, and volumes. The customer profile and the transaction profile must be crosschecked against the client's actual activities to ensure provided information and the actual business activities match and make sense for that particular client.

c. Transaction monitoring

Financial institutions must monitor the transactions carried out by their clients by using automation to identify potentially suspect transactions. The account or customer activity should be monitored for significant changes, and financial institutions should look for changes inconsistent with the legitimate normal business of the customer.

The financial institution's monitoring procedures should focus on high-risk clients, source of significant funds, and transactions that are inconsistent with the transaction profile. When inquiring about the clients' source of funds, the financial institution should examine the method (cash, check, and wire), the name of the sending financial institution, and the event that caused the funds to become available (i.e. sale of land, etc).

When abnormal and/or suspicious activity, if any, is identified, it must be reported to the respective local authorities.

Appendix 1 shows a sample customer and transaction profile.

d. Dealing with other financial institutions

Financial institutions should pay closer attention when dealing with entities that conduct financial transactions for their own customers (This type of customers would include banks, brokers or dealers in securities, money transmitters, currency exchanges, foreign exchange businesses, issuers and sellers of money orders, travelers' checks, mutual funds, as well as attorney escrow accounts, and hotels with casinos). When this is the case, the KYC program should be expanded to cover the customers of the entity that conducts transactions for its own customers, a concept known as Know Your Customers' Customers (KYCC). The financial institutions anti-money laundering and anti-terrorists financing policy should require additional anti-money laundering due diligence in these cases. Generally, financial institutions cannot know their customer's customers, so they must be assured such entities have reasonable KYC policies and procedures to protect themselves from money launderers and terrorists.

There are two possible scenarios here. The first scenario deals with customers domiciled in countries that have local anti-money laundering and anti-terrorists financing laws applicable to the customers' business activity, and which have demonstrated that they enforce these laws. In this case, the financial institution must confirm, through discussions with management, that the client has internal policies, procedures, and staff training that enable it to comply with the relevant local laws. This discussion must be documented together with a description of the client's principal anti-money laundering and anti-terrorists financing policies and procedures, and the financial institution should confirm there is no information in the marketplace that would cause it to question the entity's assurances.

The second scenario deals with customers domiciled in countries that do not have local anti-money laundering and anti-terrorists financing laws applicable to the customer's business activity or in countries that have such laws but do not have a record of enforcing these laws. Under this scenario, the financial institution must obtain reasonable assurance, through discussions with management, that the customer is aware of the risks of money laundering, terrorists financing and of the extensive legal and regulatory requirements imposed by the FATF countries, and that the financial institution will expect the customer's cooperation in the event it detects suspicious transactions in their account. This discussion must be documented together with the financial institution's explanation of the nature and quality of the client's customer base, and a confirmation that there is no information in the marketplace that would cause it to be concerned that the client was engaging in or being used for money laundering or terrorists financing. Such accounts are to be risk assessed and monitored in the same way as all other accounts.

e. Enhanced due diligence program

Some higher risk customers (private bank clients, high net worth clients, etc.) may require enhanced due diligence. In such case, the financial institution should conduct an assessment of the customers to determine the amount of enhanced due diligence required. At a minimum, financial institutions should have procedures in place that accomplish the following:

➢ Identification and verification of the customer
➢ Understanding the customer relationship with the financial institution
➢ More intensified monitoring of the accounts, and

> Identification and reporting of suspicious transactions to local authorities.

f. Terrorist financing monitoring

In addition to the implementation of the above five KYC elements financial institutions should perform the below minimum guidelines which will help them detect possible financing of terrorists:

> Financial institutions must have an automated mechanism to monitor transactions that may possibly be conducted by designated (by the United Nations or local governments) terrorists or terrorist groups.
> Financial institutions must specifically monitor funds transfers made by their clients so as to detect any unusual activity.
> Financial institutions should not enter into any transaction knowing that terrorists or terrorist groups own the funds or the property involved or that the transaction is linked to terrorism.
> Financial institutions must report suspicious transactions of any individual or entity to competent authorities.
> In line with the FATF Nine Special Recommendations on terrorist financing, financial institutions must obtain the details of the remitter's name, account number, address, purpose of the transfer, etc., conducting outgoing funds transfers.
> Financial institutions must also oversee and monitor the activities of all charity and non-profit organizations.

Furthermore, financial institutions should pay close attention to the following list of indicators that may possibly indicate that the transactions may be related to terrorist activities:

> Sudden movement over inactive accounts
> Customer refusal to provide information
> Accounts with several authorized signatories
> Accounts with many small deposits and few funds transfers
> Cash withdrawals by account holders who do not usually conduct cash transactions
> Transactions conducted using several tellers and branches

- ➤ Persons who serve as directors for multiple companies located in the same area
- ➤ Accounts opened in the name of recently established entities where higher than expected deposits are made that are not in line with the net worth of the founders.
- ➤ Opening of multiple accounts by one person where small deposits are made but which in aggregate are not in line with the income of the client.
- ➤ Accounts opened in the name of legal entities involved in activities related to terrorist organization identified by the Untied Nations or the local government.
- ➤ Structuring deposits through multiple branches of the same financial institution or deposits made by many individuals into the same account, at the same time and at the same branch
- ➤ Transactions that fall just under central bank reporting limits
- ➤ The usage of accounts of non-profit organizations or charities to collect donations and then remitting the funds to foreign beneficiaries
- ➤ Unemployed or self-employed persons making cash transactions that are not in line with their anticipated activities
- ➤ An unemployed individual receiving or sending wire transfers, or making daily cash withdrawals at multiple branches
- ➤ Charity organizations conducting financial transactions where there appears to be no linkage between the activity of the organization and the other parties of the transaction
- ➤ Foreign currency exchange transactions followed by wire transfers to countries designated by FATF as non-cooperative countries and territories
- ➤ Accounts opened for entities in FATF list of non-cooperative countries and territories

A process to identify high-risk accounts[13]

A process to identify high-risk customers for ongoing transaction monitoring and enhanced due diligence must be developed. The

---

[13] The classification of accounts into low or high-risk is discussed in more details under Classification of Accounts.

KYC and enhanced due diligence program should be based upon a risk based approach. The key factors to consider in developing appropriate controls to manage money laundering and terrorists financing risk are the different categories of customers, the localities of the businesses and customers, the nature of the products and services provided, and the expected use by customers of products and services. Some of the categories considered routine and usual are:

- Low aggregate balance accounts
- Household accounts
- Low volume of activity
- Accounts for minors
- Savings and/or checking accounts
- Other similar type accounts

These would require routine identification and verification but are low risk and would not require enhanced due diligence. These customers can be monitored en masse using exception reports or product parameters to detect a particular customer who steps outside the normal activity for the group. These accounts would be subject, however, to the minimum standards for identification and verification as required under applicable laws.

For example, most banks have procedures to monitor their account base for cash transactions. If one of the types of accounts above started to exhibit cash deposit or withdrawal activity that exceeded normal thresholds, then the account would be flagged for review at that point to determine what was taking place.

Customers' categories that pose a higher risk for the financial institution, on the other hand, and should thus require more attention include:

- Private banking
- Offshore clients
- Correspondent banking (foreign and domestic)
- Politically Exposed Persons (PEP) and related individuals.
- Accounts with frequent or excessive use of funds transfers
- Funds in and out

> Frequent purchase of bank drafts just under central banks reporting limits

These categories have been identified as posing a higher risk for money laundering by regulators, and in many cases, regulatory guidance already exists for these types of accounts or businesses.

The forth category, Politically Exposed Persons (PEPs), poses a unique reputational risk for financial institutions and should thus be examined more carefully. A PEP can be defined as an individual who occupies, is actively seeking, or is being considered for, a senior position in a government or government-controlled entities of a country. A related individual of the PEP is an immediate family member of the PEP, e.g. spouse, a child, or a close associate of the PEP.

Financial institutions must make an assessment and document any reputational or other risks posed through association with Politically Exposed Persons and related individuals to determine those identified for purposes of enhanced scrutiny. Financial institutions should have policies and procedures for opening or continuing to maintain a relationship for a PEP or related individual. At a minimum, such policies should include:

> Inquiry as to the reputation of the PEP or related individual
> Review of public information regarding the PEP or related individual, such as news articles and documentation of any significant information obtained as a result of such inquiry
> Consultation with the financial institution's legal counsel
> Approval to open accounts for the PEP or related individual by senior management.
> Appropriate methods of monitoring the PEP and/or the related individual accounts

The higher the risk classification or score, the more information and verification should be required on the front end at account opening. For example, when looking at accounts for individuals, it would be expected to have a higher level of KYC and enhanced due diligence for a private banking client than a plain vanilla retail account.

High-risk customers should also be the focus and priority for ongoing monitoring efforts.

Identifying and reporting suspicious transactions to government authorities

The anti-money laundering and anti-terrorists financing policies should require the financial institution to satisfy any local legal obligations to report suspicious activity and should establish a uniform standard to determine whether transactions are suspicious. The financial institution should ensure the transaction conducted or attempted at or through it, does not involve a central bank reporting limit, and that the financial institution does not know, suspect, or has reason to suspect that the transaction:

A. Involves funds from illegal activities
B. Hides funds or assets derived from illegal activities
C. Is designed to evade a money laundering regulation
D. Has no business or apparent lawful purpose
E. Is not the sort in that the customer would normally be expected to engage

This standard establishes a threshold to report suspicious activity. It basically comes down to whether a transaction makes sense for a particular customer to engage in or if there is no reasonable explanation for the transaction. Otherwise, it should be considered suspicious under the financial institution's anti-money laundering and anti-terrorist financing policy. In making a determination as to the validity of a customer, there are certain categories of activities that are suspicious in nature and should alert financial institutions to the potential for the customer to conduct illegal activities at the institution. The categories broadly defined are:

> Insufficient, false, or inconsistent information provided by the customer
> Cash deposits or other activity that is not consistent with the business activities of the customer.
> Purchase and/or deposits of cash equivalents (e.g., traveler's checks, money orders) that are not consistent with the business activities of the customer
> Wire transfer activity that is not consistent with the business activities or financial situation of the customer
> Structuring of transactions to evade record keeping and/or central banks reporting requirements
> Unusual funds transfers to foreign countries

Consideration should be made to the use of an automated anti-money laundering solution to detect suspicious money laundering and terrorist activities. Such a system must have the following features at minimum:

> Transactions monitoring covering all areas of business including consumer, corporate, private clients, brokerage, and wholesale banking
> The ability to monitor and analyze every transaction that flows through the organization
> Ability to find those transactions that are unusual and then determining which merit attention
> Techniques for creating customer profiles and peer groups matching
> Pattern recognition—that is, ability to indicate transactions that deviate from the client's normal activity.
> Ability to detect unknown relationships between entities

> ➢ Capability to use previously identified suspicious and abnormal activities to determine the probability of reoccurrence of any current or future suspicious activity.

Financial institution with international presence

For financial institutions that have global presence, attention must be paid to countries that do not have the same requirements regarding suspicious activity similar to that of their home country. In some countries in which financial institutions operate, there is no requirement to report suspicious activity. Therefore, the financial institution's anti-money laundering and anti-terrorists financing policy should establish a uniform standard for reporting suspicious activities. For instance, a limit of 10,000 United States dollars can be established for monitoring and internal reporting purposes. All branches of the financial institution, wherever located, are to use this standard to determine whether an activity is suspicious for purposes of internal referrals to appropriate personnel as directed by their business procedures so that appropriate action is taken. This standard to identify and report suspicious activity is consistent with the forty anti-money laundering recommendations of FATF.

Staff training

Financial institutions should provide anti-money laundering and combating terrorism financing training to their staff throughout the financial institution on periodic basis to increase their awareness. The training should cover all applicable local and international laws and the laws of the countries where the institution does business.

Training should include money laundering and terrorist's financing recent trends and the financial institution's policies and procedures to combat money laundering and terrorism financing. The training should also focus on the recognition and reporting of suspicious activities.

Internal control functions and reviews of anti-money laundering policies

The financial institution's internal audit and business and compliance units should carry out independent internal reviews of the institution's anti-money laundering and combating terrorists financing policies and procedures in order to self-assess their functionality. The financial institution's audit team, or any other equivalent unit, should review the institution's compliance with its anti-money laundering, anti-terrorists financing compliance program, and with the applicable laws and regulations. The institution should also implement a self-assessment and testing mechanism to provide assurances that its anti-money laundering and combating terrorist's financing programs function well and will continue to function appropriately and effectively.

Needless to say, financial institutions that demonstrate effective implementation of the anti-money laundering and the anti-terrorists financing policies including the six KYC elements may face lesser consequences. In specific:

➢ Punitive fines may significantly decrease under sentencing guidelines if the financial institution has taken steps prior to the offence to prevent and detect criminal conduct and to co-operate with the government.
➢ If the financial institution has additionally detected and reported the criminal violation, it can reduce its exposure.

Classification of accounts

The anti-money laundering program should focus on high-risk customers the identification of which is based on red flags[14] that represent clues to which customers warrant additional attention. Red flags depend on three factors: the geography of the account, the business the client is conducting, and the products and services the client is using along with their anticipated usage.

Let's examine each area more.

High-risk geographies

These are countries that are known to have crucial anti-money laundering and terrorists financing concerns. In general, such countries include:

➤ Drug producing nations
➤ Drug transshipment countries
➤ Drug using countries
➤ Secrecy jurisdictions and tax havens, particularly those that grant offshore banking licenses

---

[14] Please refer to the Red Flags section.

> Countries identified by governments or FATF as non-cooperative jurisdictions
> Countries with a high degree of public corruption
> Countries linked to terrorist financing

Money launderers and terrorists target countries with:

1. Failure to criminalize money laundering and terrorists financing from all serious crimes or limiting the offences to narrow predicates
2. Weak central banks with inadequate supervision
3. Limited controls on foreign exchange
4. Rigid bank secrecy rules that obstruct law enforcement investigations or that prohibit or inhibit large value and/or suspicious transaction reporting by financial institutions
5. No record keeping or reporting requirements for large cash transactions
6. No mandatory suspicious transaction reporting process; lack of uniform guidelines for identifying suspicious activity
7. Inadequate KYC requirements to open accounts or conduct financial transactions
8. No asset forfeiture laws
9. Lack of effective monitoring of cross-border currency movements
10. No requirements to maintain financial records over a specific time
11. Use of bearer payable monetary instruments
12. No requirement to disclose the beneficial owner of an account or the true beneficiary of a transaction
13. Well-established non-bank financial systems, especially where regulation, supervision, and monitoring are absent or lax
14. Patterns of evasion of exchange controls by legitimate businesses

Other countries can have comprehensive laws on the books and conduct aggressive anti-money laundering and anti-terrorists financing enforcement efforts but still be classified a primary concern jurisdiction in terms of money laundering and terrorists financing (e.g., the United States or the United Kingdom). In some cases, this classification may simply or largely be a function of the size of the economy. In such jurisdictions, the volume of money laundering is likely to be substantial, necessitating quick, continuous, and effective anti-money laundering efforts by the government.

The classification of an account as high-risk based on the geography of the accounts depends on whether the country is on a high-risk list published by the government where the financial institution is located, the FATF list of Non-Cooperative Countries, OECD Harmful Tax Practices[15], Transparency International Corruption Index[16], Drug Production and Transit from the United States Department of State International Narcotics Control Strategy Report (INCSR),[17] or a country linked to terrorism.

High-risk businesses:

Money launderers have traditionally used the businesses listed below because they provide a good cover or seemingly legitimate explanation for the illicit proceeds:

1. Non-bank financial entities such as currency exchange houses also known as *giros* or *casas de cambio*, money transmitters, and check cashing facilities
2. Banks located in areas designated as high intensity drug trafficking areas by the United States Office of the National Drug Control Policy[18]

---

[15] An OECD drive to improve cooperation with jurisdictions identified as tax havens. OECD publishes a *Framework for a Collective Memorandum of Understanding on Eliminating Harmful Tax Practices*—which it hopes could form a basis for the OECD to continue its dialogue with these jurisdictions.

[16] The Global Corruption Index is an annual evaluation of the state of corruption around the world, produced by Transparency International, the world's leading anti-corruption Non-Government Organization. The report draws together analyses from experts and journalists and presents recent developments in both corruption and the fight against it.

[17] INCSR provides the factual basis for the Presidential narcotics certification determinations for major drug producing and/or drug transit countries

[18] The Office of National Drug Control Policy is a component of the Executive Office of the United States President. Its principal purpose is to establish policies, priorities, and objectives for the drug control program. The goals of the program are to reduce illicit drug use, manufacturing, and trafficking, drug related crime and violence, and drug related health consequences.

3. Casinos, gaming establishments, and card clubs
4. Offshore subsidiaries of corporations and banks located in tax and/or secrecy havens
5. Leather goods stores
6. Car, boat, and plane dealerships
7. Used automobile, truck, and machine parts manufacturers
8. Travel agencies
9. Broker dealers
10. Jewel, gem, and precious metal dealers
11. Import, export, and trading companies
12. Cash intensive businesses (restaurants, convenience stores, parking garages, etc.)
13. Telemarketers
14. Wholesalers and retailers of consumer electronics (particularly in free trade zones)
15. Textile businesses
16. Sole practitioner
17. Small or little known law firms, accountants, or investment brokers
18. Art and antique dealers
19. Real estate brokers and agents
20. Costume jewelry exporters
21. Pawn brokers
22. Auctioneers
23. Ship, bus, and plane operators
24. Charitable organizations

In evaluating business risk, financial institutions also need to consider whether the client will have cross border transactions and/or will be dealing with customers in other high-risk countries, whether the business is cash intensive, whether the business will conduct financial transactions on behalf of third parties (check cashers, money remitters, etc.), and whether it is subject to regulation or other oversight.

In the case of high-risk businesses, the base protection is an actual site visit to the customer's premises to ensure it exists and to verify and observe the level of activity.

Visits should be documented in writing.

High-risk products and services

Products and services that permit cash conversion are considered to be high-risk products. Travelers' checks, cashier's checks, bank drafts, money orders, and electronic funds transfers are examples. The tremendous volume and anonymity provided by the electronic funds transfer network makes this product attractive to launderers and terrorists. They can move funds by wire around the globe in few hours. The more jurisdictions involved, the harder it will be to trace the funds.

Any product which allows a customer to readily convert cash to a monetary instrument or move value from one jurisdiction to another and which conceals the source of those funds should be classified as a high-risk product and/or service.

To mitigate this risk, financial institutions must determine whether the products or services the client is asking for make sense given the nature of their account or business. At the end of the day, the products and services request should fit with the nature of the business or the financial situation of the customer.

Examples of high-risk services:

1. Electronic banking that permits customers direct and online access to transact
2. Private banking relationships
3. Services to Politically Exposed Persons and related individuals
4. Private investment companies
5. Payable through accounts
6. Trusts
7. International correspondent banking activity
8. Transactions involving a financial intermediary where the primary beneficiary or counterparty is undisclosed
9. Trade financing with unusual (overvalued or undervalued) pricing and invoicing

Clients in high-risk businesses (e.g. travel agencies or charity organization), located in high-risk geographies (e.g. Turkey or the United States, etc.), and using high-risk products and services (e.g. checks or letters of credit) must be classified as high-risk accounts and must be subject to more intensified monitoring and should require more extensive due diligence. In addition, decisions to enter into business with higher risk customer should be taken at the senior management levels.

Red flags

Because money laundering and terrorists activities have been around for many years, international law enforcement agencies have had plenty of time to study the patterns and techniques used by money launderers and terrorists, and they have, as a result, been able to come up with a list of red flags of possible money laundering activities. Red flags can be defined as clues (indicators or warning signs) or triggers of suspicion to which financial institutions need to pay additional attention.

Red flags take into consideration the three risk classifications discussed earlier (high-risk geography, high-risk businesses, and high-risk products and services). If a red flag is located, it should immediately trigger suspicion to the financial institution. The financial institution should investigate the matter further, and if suspicions do prove warranted, they must be reported to the financial institution's anti-money laundering and combating terrorists financing officer who is fully authorized to take action on cases where money-laundering activity is suspected.

If the anti-money laundering and combating terrorists financing officer determines that suspicions are true, he or she must then involve the proper law enforcement and/or regulatory officials at the proper time.

Red flags are listed below at several areas of the financial institutions, which by no means is an exclusive list.

Tellers and customer service personnel

> ➢ Customer is reluctant to provide any information requested for proper identification
> ➢ Customer opens a number of accounts under one or more names and subsequently makes deposits of less than a central bank reporting limit in cash in each of the accounts
> ➢ Customer is reluctant to proceed with a transaction after being informed that a Currency Transaction Report will be filed, or withholds information necessary to complete the form
> ➢ Customer makes frequent deposits or withdrawals of large amounts of currency for no apparent business reason or for a business that generally does not involve large amounts of cash
> ➢ Customer exchanges large amounts of currency from small to large denomination bills
> ➢ Customer makes frequent purchases of cash equivalents for cash in amounts less than a central bank reporting limit with different tellers
> ➢ Customers enter the bank simultaneously and each conducts a large currency transaction under a central bank reporting limit with different tellers
> ➢ Customer makes constant deposits of funds into an account and almost immediately requests wire transfers to another city or country, and that activity is inconsistent with the customer's stated business
> ➢ A review of checks paid against uncollected funds indicates that the customer is offsetting checks with deposits of the same or similar amount and maintains a relatively constant account balance, usually small in relation to the amount of activity and size of the transactions
> ➢ Customer receives wire transfers and immediately purchases cash equivalents for payment to another party
> ➢ Traffic patterns of a customer change in the safe deposit box area, possibly indicating the safekeeping of large amounts of cash
> ➢ Customer discusses Currency Transaction Report filing requirements with the apparent intention of avoiding those re-

quirements or makes threats to an employee to deter the filing of one.

➤ Customer requests to be exempted from the Currency Transaction Report filing.

Wire transfer operations

➤ Customer experiences increased wire activity when previously there has been no regular wire activity

➤ International transfers for customer accounts with no history of such transfers or where the stated business of the customer does not warrant such activity

➤ Customer receives many small incoming wire transfers or deposits of checks and money orders then requests wire transfers to another city or country

➤ Customer uses wire transfers to move large amounts of money to a bank secrecy haven country (such as Switzerland)

➤ Request from a non-accountholder to receive or send wire transfers involving currency from non-accountholder near a central bank reporting limit or that involves numerous cash equivalents.

➤ Non-accountholder receives incoming wire transfers under instructions to the bank to pay upon proper identification or to convert the funds to cashier's checks and mail them to the non-accountholder.

Loan officers

➤ Customer's stated purpose for the loan does not make economic sense, or customer proposes that cash collateral be provided for a loan while refusing to disclose the purpose of loan

➤ Customer requests loans to offshore companies, or loans secured by obligations of offshore banks

➤ Borrower pays down a large problem loan suddenly with no reasonable explanation of the source of funds

➤ Customer purchases certificates of deposit and uses them as loan collateral

➤ Customer collateralizes a loan with a cash deposit

➤ Customer uses cash collateral located offshore to obtain a loan
➤ Loan proceeds are unexpectedly channeled offshore
➤ Purpose of loan is not recorded
➤ Proceeds of loan are used for a purpose other than that recorded

Offshore transactions

➤ Loans made on the strength of a borrower's financial statement reflect major investments in and income from businesses incorporated in bank secrecy haven countries
➤ Transactions involving an offshore shell bank whose name may be very similar to the name of a major legitimate institution
➤ Offers of multi-million dollar deposits at below market rates from a confidential source to be sent from or somehow guaranteed by an offshore bank through a letter, telex, or other official communication
➤ Presence of telex or facsimile equipment where the usual and customary business activity would not appear to justify the need for such equipment

Wire transfers

➤ Indications of frequent overrides of established approval authority and other internal controls
➤ Intentional circumvention of approval authority by splitting transactions
➤ In a linked financing situation, a borrower requests the immediate wire transfer of loan proceeds to a number of banks where the funds for the brokered deposits originated.
➤ Large or frequent wire transfers against uncollected funds
➤ Customer complaints and/or frequent error conditions

Financing and brokered transactions

➤ Out-of-territory lending
➤ Loan production used as a basis for officer bonuses

➢ Evidence of unsolicited attempts to buy or recapitalize the bank where there is evidence of a request for large loans at or about the same time by persons previously unknown to the bank; promises of large dollar deposits may also be involved

➢ Promise of large dollar deposits in consideration for favorable treatment on loan requests

➢ Brokerage deposit transactions where the broker's fees are paid for from the proceeds of related loans

➢ Anytime a bank seriously considers a loan request where the bank would have to obtain brokered deposits to be able to fund the loan should be viewed with suspicion

➢ Solicitations by persons who purportedly have access to multi-millions of dollars from a confidential source readily available for loans and/or deposits in a financial institution, particularly where the rates and terms quoted are substantially more favorable than those available through normal sources; a substantial fee may be requested in advance or the solicitor may suggest that the fee be paid at closing and demand compensation for expenses, often exceeding 50,000 dollars

➢ Prepayment of interest on deposit accounts where such deposit accounts are used as collateral for loans

Credit cards and electronic funds transfers

➢ Poor control of credit limit increases

➢ Poor control of name and address changes

➢ Frequent malfunction of payment authorization system

➢ Unusual delays in receipt of cards and Personal Identification Numbers (PIN) by the customers

➢ Bank does not limit amount of cash that a customer can extract from an Automated Teller Machine (ATM) in a given day

➢ Evidence that a merchant has intentionally structured customer credit card purchases to keep individual amounts below the floor limit to avoid the need for transaction approval

➢ Prepayment of non-existing balances often followed by closing the account with a request for the bank to send a check

Real estate investment

➤ When there are traces or signs that customers are not acting on their own behalf, trying to conceal the true beneficiary's identity

➤ Purchases of real estate using false names

➤ Investment in tourist or recreational real estate complexes such as hotels or golf courses, particularly when funded from offshore

➤ Purchases by third parties or intermediaries (fiduciaries)

➤ Multiple purchases by the same individual without a reasonable explanation

➤ Real estate investments by non-residents

➤ Real estate purchases on behalf of minors

➤ Real estate transactions conducted by the same or related persons that occur within a short period of time

➤ High value real estate transactions conducted by companies with small available capital for investments

➤ Transactions with persons with unknown addresses, post office addresses, or who provide insufficient or false information

➤ Transactions using shell companies as middlemen, especially those domiciled in secrecy havens

➤ Foreign buyers whose presence in the country is just to close the transaction

➤ Unusual haste to close a real estate transaction

➤ Real estate investments using funds booked in tax havens or high-risk countries

➤ Impulse purchases or those without sufficient justification

➤ Trust corporations established in tax havens used as partners, estate agents, or investors

➤ Purchases made by residents on behalf of non-residents or non-residents on behalf of residents

➤ Transactions done by several individuals and companies without clear relationship, usually on behalf of a non-resident third party

➤ Real estate transactions conducted in cash or with other cash equivalents such as travelers' checks or money orders

Third party obligations

> Incomplete documentation on guarantees
> Lack of credit information on third party obligor
> Financial statements reflect concentrations of closely held companies or businesses that lack audited financial statements to support their value

Securities, insurance, and investment

> The customer refuses or is reluctant to complete an application to provide all the required information, or the information provided is false or suspicious in nature
> The customer attempts to purchase an insurance policy or annuity or to make an investment in an amount that is far beyond his, her, or its apparent means, and that has no obvious purpose, or where the source or nature of the funds to be used is suspicious
> The customer wishes to buy an investment or insurance product but is less concerned with the long-term performance or the economic terms than in early surrender or cancellation.
> The customer does not appear to be concerned about the cost of a policy or an annuity or in determining the suitability of the product to his, her, or its needs
> The customer seeks to make purchases or investments with large amounts of cash or by making any other large payments with cash
> The customer makes payments for insurance or investment products with numerous cash equivalents, with checks drawn on different accounts, or checks drawn on an account other than his, her, or its own
> The customer seeks to purchase a single premium policy or annuity or to prepay the premiums and thereafter borrow the maximum cash value or use the policy or annuity as collateral for a loan
> The customer seeks to cancel a life insurance policy during the free look period or prior to maturity without regard to penalties

- The customer demands policy loan or surrender value quickly
- There appears to be no apparent relationship between the owner and the insured, annuitant, or beneficiary
- The customer receives wired funds followed by a request for immediate disbursement by cash, check, or wire to a third party
- The customer deposits bearer bonds followed by immediate sale and wire out of the proceeds
- The customer receives funds that do not correspond with the customer's known business activities and financial situation
- The customer requests disbursements of large sums of cash or attempts to deposit large sums of cash, money orders, or travelers cheques
- The customer requests repeated exceptions to policies relating to deposits
- The customer deposits several cashiers' checks, all in amounts under a central bank reporting limit or in amounts just under the local cash recording and reporting requirements overseas
- The customer establishes an investment account but appears unconcerned about the usual decisions to be made regarding an investment account such as fees, investment objectives, suitable investment vehicles, and so on

Trade services

- Transaction does not provide for a description of the goods or technology being shipped.
- Changing the letter of credit beneficiary name and address just before payment is to be made including assignment of proceeds or transfers at the time documents are presented
- Changing the letter of credit place of payment. That is, payment is to be made to beneficiary's account held in another country other than the beneficiary's stated location
- Commercial letter of credit or collection purportedly covering the movement of goods but fails to call for presentation of transport documents

➤ Transfer or assignment of proceeds that reflects an unusual profit margin in the transaction or names an offshore financial haven

➤ Standby letter of credit used as bid bonds or performance bonds without normal reference to an underlying project or contract or in favor of an unusual beneficiary (except for insurance related letters of credit where the letter of credit calls for a draft only. This is an acceptable insurance industry practice)

➤ Commercial letters of credit that allow payment to be requested from a bank by a beneficiary in the same country without presentation of documents to be sent directly to the issuing bank (Note: When the beneficiary is outside the paying bank's country, sending documents through the paying bank may cause delays.)

➤ International transactions for customer or accounts with no history of such transactions or when the stated business of the customer does not warrant such activity

➤ Unusually favorable payment terms, such as payment far above or below market price, interest rate far above or below prevailing rate, or lump sum cash payment

➤ Transaction involves an unusual intermediary or number of intermediaries

➤ Insufficient, false, or suspicious information provided by the customer

➤ Letters of credit for large amounts involving high-risk countries

➤ Bill of lading not consigned or consignment is to be advised between the applicant and beneficiary. Consignment should be to a named party (usually the applicant, broker, bank, or to the order of shipper blank endorsed)

➤ Customer requests an unusual degree of confidentiality or deviation from the bank's established process with respect to the transaction.

➤ Approach from previously unknown customer whose identity is not clear, who appears evasive about his/her identity or connections, or whose references are not convincing

- Customer reluctant to provide clear answers to routine financial, commercial, technical, or other questions
- Bill of lading describing containerized cargo without container numbers or with sequential numbers.

Politically Exposed Persons (PEP) and related individuals:

While the following red flags pertain to Politically Exposed Persons and related individuals, many of them are applicable to other types of customers as well.

- A Politically Exposed Person or related individual requests to establish a relationship with, or route transactions through, a financial institution or a department or branch of a financial institution that does not usually do business with foreign persons and that does not seek foreign business
- A Politically Exposed Person or related individual seeks to make his or her financial activity more secretive or difficult to trace, such as by requesting that transactions be booked in the name of another person or a business entity or be routed through an account in the name of the financial institution, such as an omnibus or concentration account
- A Politically Exposed Person or related individual requests that transactions be moved to or through a secrecy jurisdiction or jurisdictions with lax money laundering controls, such as FATF Non-Cooperative Countries and Territories
- A Politically Exposed Person or related individual requests that funds be routed through several jurisdictions and/or financial institutions prior to or following entry of funds into an institution in a certain country without any apparent purpose other than to disguise the nature, source, ownership, or control of the funds
- Funds are sent to an account of a Politically Exposed Person or related individual from accounts in a nation's central bank, other government-owned bank, or from a government account
- There is a rapid increase or decrease in the funds or asset value in an account of a Politically Exposed Person or related indi-

98

vidual that is not attributable to fluctuations in the market value of investments held in the account

➢ There is frequent or excessive use of funds transfers or wire transfers in or out of an account

➢ Originator information is not provided in payment orders for wire transfers to or for the benefit of a Politically Exposed Person or related individual when inclusion of such information would be expected

➢ Deposits or withdrawals are made involving large amounts of currency or bearer instruments.

➢ Deposits or withdrawals are made with multiple monetary instruments with face values just below a central bank record keeping or reporting thresholds

➢ Large deposits or withdrawals are made in amounts not commensurate with the type of account or what is known regarding the legitimate wealth, income, or business of the Politically Exposed Person or related individual

➢ There is a pattern of deposits to the account of a Politically Exposed Person or related individual followed shortly by requests for wire transfers out of the account, especially if the transfer is to an account in a secrecy jurisdiction or other high-risk jurisdiction for money laundering

➢ A minimal balance is maintained or the account is zeroed out for purposes other than maximizing the value of the funds held in the account.

➢ The Politically Exposed Person or related individual makes inquiries regarding exceptions to the central bank record keeping or reporting requirements, including the Suspicious Activity Report requirement, or the financial institution's anti-money laundering and anti-terrorists financing policies and procedures.

Other

➢ Increases in cash shipments that are not accompanied by a corresponding increase in the number of accounts

➢ Cash on hand frequently exceeds limits established in security program and/or insurance coverage

- ➤ Large volumes of cashiers' checks, money orders, or travelers' cheques are sold for cash
- ➤ Accounts have a large number of small deposits and a small number of large checks with the balance of the account remaining relatively low and constant. Account has many of the same characteristics as an account at the same bank or at another bank
- ➤ Large volumes of cashiers' checks or money orders are deposited to an account where the nature of the account holder's business would not appear to justify such activity.
- ➤ Cash deposits to a correspondent bank account by any means other than through an armored carrier
- ➤ Cash shipments that appear large in comparison to the dollar volume of Currency Transaction Reports filed
- ➤ Dollar limits on the list of bank customers exempt from currency transaction reporting requirements that appear unreasonably high considering the type and location of the business with insufficient information in the bank's files to support the limits set
- ➤ Currency Transaction Reports, when filed, are often incorrect or lack important information
- ➤ List of exempted customers appears unusually long

Self-assessment Checklist

This self-assessment questionnaire (using FATF methodology) will assist financial institutions to determine the degree to which they have implemented measures to fight money laundering and terrorists financing. Financial institutions should fairly respond to all questions so as to see where they stand in terms of meeting the international and local anti-money laundering and combating terrorism financing standards and requirements.

Country's Legal System

1. Does confidentiality, secrecy law, agreement, or any other law inhibit the implementation of the criteria set out in this book?
2. Has the country designated competent authorities to ensure effective implementation of the FAFT Forty and Nine Special Recommendations?

Customer Identification

1. Do financial institutions identify the person or entity that maintains an account with them or those on whose behalf an account is maintained (beneficial owners), the beneficiaries of transactions conducted by professional intermediaries; and any person or entity connected with a financial transaction

who pose a significant reputational or other risk to the financial institution?

2. Do financial institutions have a systematic procedure for identifying customers, and do they not open accounts until the identity of the customer has been satisfactorily verified?

3. Do financial institutions pay special attention to non-resident customers and understand the reasons for which the customer has chosen to open an account in a foreign country?

4. Do financial institutions have an enhanced due diligence for private banking operations?

5. Do financial institutions apply enhanced diligence for a customer if they, for any reason, believe the customer is being refused facilities by another financial institution?

6. When an account has been opened, do financial institutions close accounts (subject to any national legislation on handling of suspicious transactions) for customers when problems of verification arise in the relationship that cannot be resolved?

7. For trust customers, do financial institutions obtain information about the trustees, settlers, grantors, and beneficiaries?

8. Do financial institutions try to understand and document the structure of corporate customers, determine the source of funds, and identify the beneficial owners and those who have control over the funds to prevent the corporate customer being used to operate anonymous accounts?

9. Do financial institutions also take special care when initiating business transactions with companies that have nominee shareholders or shares in bearer form?

Using Introducers

1. When financial institutions use introducers, does the responsibility for knowing the customer remain with the financial institution?

2. If financial institutions rely on the introducer for KYC purposes, do they use the following conditions to determine whether they can rely on introducers?

➢ The introducer complies with the minimum customer due diligence standards required by the financial institution
➢ The customer due diligence procedures of the introducer are as rigorous as those which the financial institution would have conducted itself for the customer
➢ The financial institution must satisfy itself as to the reliability of the systems put in place by the introducer to verify the identity of the customer
➢ The introducer to the financial institution immediately submits all relevant identification date and other documentation pertaining to the customer's identity

Professional Intermediaries

1. Do financial institutions identify the beneficial owners of client accounts opened by professional intermediaries?
2. Is this process subject to the following conditions?

➢ The intermediary is subject to the same regulatory and money laundering legislation and procedures and the same customer due diligence standards in respect of its client base, as the financial institution
➢ The financial institution is able to establish that the intermediary has engaged in a sound due diligence process
➢ The intermediary is able to allocate the assets in the pooled accounts to the relevant beneficiaries
➢ The intermediary is able to furnish the required information on beneficiaries to the financial institution

Politically Exposed Persons

Do the financial institutions have policy and procedures for handling customer relationships with Politically Exposed Persons and do such policies cover:

➢ Identification of PEP among new or existing customers
➢ Identification of persons or companies related to the PEP
➢ Verification of the sources of funds prior to account opening

> ➤ Senior management approval for establishing relationship with the PEP

Corruption

Do financial institutions accept or maintain a business relationship if they know or must assume that the funds derive from corruption of public assets, without prejudice to any obligation the financial institution has under criminal law or other laws or regulations?

Non-account holders

Do financial institutions equally apply effective customer identification procedures for non-face-to-face customers as for those available for interview, and are there specific and adequate measures to mitigate the higher risk?

Correspondent accounts

1. Do financial institutions have policies and procedures regarding the opening of correspondent accounts?
2. Do such procedures, at the minimum, require the financial institution to:

   > ➤ fully understand and document the nature of the respondent financial institution management and business;
   > ➤ maintain that the respondent financial institution has effective customer acceptance and KYC policies and is effectively supervised;
   > ➤ identify and monitor the use of correspondent accounts that may be used as payable through accounts; and
   > ➤ not enter into or continue a correspondent relationship with a financial institution incorporated in a jurisdiction in which it has no physical presence and which is unaffiliated with a regulated financial group (i.e. shell financial institutions)?

Ongoing monitoring of accounts and transactions

1. Are financial institutions able to aggregate and monitor significant balances and activity in customer accounts on a fully consolidated worldwide basis, regardless of whether the accounts are held on balance sheet, off balance sheet, as assets under management, or in a fiduciary basis?
2. Do financial institutions have systems in place to detect unusual or suspicious patterns of activities in all accounts, such as significant transactions relative to a relationship, transactions that exceed certain limits, very high account turnover inconsistent with the size of the balance, or transactions which fall out of the regular pattern of the account's activity?
3. Do financial institutions conduct intensified monitoring of high-risk accounts?
4. Do financial institutions pay particular attention when continuing relationships with another financial institution located in jurisdiction that have poor KYC standards or have been identified as being non-cooperative in the fight against anti-money laundering and terrorists financing?
5. Are financial institutions required to pay particular attention to transactions involving such jurisdictions?
6. Do financial institutions give scrutiny to wire transfers that do not contain complete originator information?

Suspicious activities

1. Do financial institutions report promptly their suspicions to financial investigation unit in a form of a suspicious activity report when they suspect that assets involved either stem from a criminal activity or are linked or related to or are to be used to finance terrorism?
2. Do financial institutions have clear procedures communicated to all personnel for reporting suspicious transactions?
3. Do financial institutions warn (tip off) their customers when information relating to them is reported to competent authorities?

Record Keeping

Do financial institutions have clear standards on what records must be kept on customer identification and individual transactions and their retention period?

Internal controls, compliance, audit, and training

1. Do financial institutions establish and maintain internal controls and procedures to prevent their institutions from being used for money laundering or terrorism financing purposes?
2. Do they have anti-money laundering and combating terrorism financing programs that include internal procedures and policies, ongoing training, and audit function to test the system to ensure adequate compliance with these programs?
3. Have financial institutions established procedures and allocated responsibilities to ensure KYC policies and procedures are managed effectively and are in line with local supervisory practice?
4. Do financial institutions have an adequately resourced compliance function which provides independent evaluation of the financial institution's own policies and procedures and is responsible for the ongoing monitoring of staff performance through sample testing of compliance and for reporting to senior management or the board of directors in case of failures in KYC procedures?
5. Do financial institutions apply an accepted minimum KYC standard policies and procedures on a global basis, covering foreign branches and subsidiaries, as well as affiliates?
6. Do financial institutions ensure that employees are kept informed of new developments, including information on current money laundering and terrorism financing techniques, methods and trends, and that there is a clear explanation of anti-money laundering and combating terrorism financing laws and obligations such as requirements for customer identification, due diligence, and suspicious activity reports?

7. Do financial institutions designate anti-money laundering and combating terrorism financing compliance officers at management level?

8. Do financial institutions put in place adequate screening to ensure high standards when hiring employees?

Summary

It is without doubt that money laundering and terrorism financing has become a key focus for many governments and lawmakers around the globe. This focus has resulted in a noticeable growth in the depth of anti-money laundering and combating terrorist financing measures. In today's world, money laundering and terrorism financing can be carried out using virtually any financial instrument that financial institutions offer. They have become very complex and thus, there is no longer a specific rule that can be used to detect and discover money laundering and terrorism financing activities.

The fight against money laundering and terrorism financing is a long battle. Money launderers and terrorists are always one step ahead of financial institutions and are continually changing their behaviors to avoid being detected and caught. Money laundering and terrorism financing undermine confidence in the international financial system. The challenges in the fight against money laundering and terrorism financing are vast, and potential threats exist in every corner of the world. Financial institutions and law enforcement agencies work hard to stay ahead of increasingly sophisticated criminals seeking to exploit the global financial system.

Money laundering has devastating social, economical, and other consequences and is a threat to all countries. It provides the fuel for drug dealers, terrorists, and other criminals to operate and expand their criminal activities. Money laundering and terrorism financing have become increasingly international in scope, and the financial aspects of them have become more complex due to rapid advances in technology and the globalization of the financial services industry.

Undetected money laundering and terrorism financing activities can erode the integrity of a nation's financial institutions. They could also adversely affect currencies and interest rates as launderers and terrorists reinvest funds where their schemes are less likely to be detected. Ultimately, laundered money flows into global financial systems, and it could undermine national economies and currencies. Money laundering is, thus, not only a law enforcement problem but poses a serious international security threat as well. In addition, money launderers negatively affect countries by reducing tax revenues through underground economies, competing unfairly with legitimate businesses, damaging financial systems, and disrupting economic development. Therefore, money laundering and terrorism financing should now be viewed as a central dilemma dealing with all forms of organized crime. Fighting money launderers and terrorist financing not only reduces financial crime, but it also deprives criminals and terrorists of the means to commit other serious crimes.

Financial institutions would always be a target for money launderers and terrorists; they must, therefore, be committed to the fight against money laundering and terrorism financing. Financial institutions must be vigilant for suspicious activities and must promptly report those to appropriate authorities within their countries. Only through continuous and constant vigilance can financial institutions and their employees protect their businesses from being used by money launderers and terrorists. At the end of the day, no customer relationship is worth compromising the financial institution's commitment to combating money laundering and the financing of terrorist activities.

Furthermore, the continued abuse of financial institutions has also enhanced the need for new technologies to combat money laundering and terrorism financing. Such technologies must be capable of detecting simple and complex money laundering and terrorism financing schemes.

It is why adherence to the policies and procedures highlighted in this book, in addition to the strict compliance with the applicable combating money laundering and terrorist financing laws and regulations, is extremely crucial to ensure the survival of financial institutions.

Appendix I - Customer Information Form (CIF)

The CIF must be completed by the account officer of the client, reviewed by the financial institution's compliance officer, and signed by the division head of the department. All questions must be answered. CIF must be updated on an annual basis.

I. UPDATE INFORMATION
Account number, currency of the account, and date opened:
II. ACCOUNT INFORMATION
Client's name:
Business address:
Mailing address:
Telephone/Fax Number:
Internet address:
Name of relationship manager and phone number:
Banking relationships at other institutions (past or present) including name and address: Has the client or been requested to close accounts with other banks? If yes, name bank and reason.

Purpose of account:

III. COMMERCIAL INFORMATION

Type of legal entity, corporation, public-sector entity, sole proprietor, partnership, limited liability company, others.
Does the client provide money orders, traveler's checks, money transmission, check cashing:

Place and date of incorpora-tion/formation:	Legal documents reviewed and year of issuance:

Any recent recent mergers, acquisitions, major changes in ownership which occurred: Any significant expected or recent changes in business activities:
Affiliates and subsidiaries
Owners name and country of legal residence
Board members and senior management (name and country of legal residence):
Market reputation of the client
Are there politically exposed persons in the ownership or management of this entity? If yes, the approval of senior management must be obtained
Contact person (Name and telephone):
Description of business operations including size of business activity, years in business, and number of employees
Primary locations:
Major suppliers and major customers:
For high-risk clients, has a site visit been made and documented:

IV FINANCIAL INFORMATION

Financial highlights: total assets, total liabilities, total annual sales/revenues, and date of financial statements:

V. ANTI-MONEY LAUNDERING—ENHANCED DUE DILIGENCE

Provide a description and assessment of the client's awareness of AML issues and any discussion you have held with management on this topic:

Anti-money laundering risk assessment:

Does the customer deal principally with customers or suppliers located in high-risk geographies?

Is the client's business a high-risk business?

Does the client use high-risk products, wire transfers, letters of credit, drafts, or traveler's checks?

If the answers are yes to all three questions, the account must be classified as high-risk.

VI. Customer Transaction Profile

Indicate all products and services that are to be delivered to the client: automated clearinghouse, disbursements, electronic banking, loans, securities, deposits, letters of credit, wire transfers.

Anticipated product activity information

Expected debits	Range of transactions and average	Value and average
E.g. Checks deposit	1-5, average 3	$1000-10,000, average 7,000
Outgoing transfers		
Drafts/Travelers checks		
Cash withdrawals		
Treasury products		
Money markets		
Loans		
Import letters of credit		
Check cashed/cleared		
Investments transactions		
Credit cards payments		
Others, specify		

Expected credits:
Cash deposits
Loans and deposits
Check deposits
Investment transactions
Incoming wire transfers
Export letters of credit
Treasury product
Others, specify

For clients conducting wire transfer activity, please indicate the nature of the activity, payments to suppliers, payments from customers, payroll payments, inter-company payments, other.

Indicate countries from/to which funds transfers are anticipated:

Is the client's anticipated activity commensurate with the client's annual sales/income?
Are there seasonal variations in volume?

VII. REFERENCES

Name of Institution	Methof of Checking	Results	

IX. REVIEW AND APPROVAL

Relationship: manager, unit head, and compliance officer (name, date, and signature):

Appendix II - 40+9 The United Nations Resolutions

United Nations Resolution 1373 (2001), Adopted by the Security Council at its 4385th meeting on 28 September 2001,

The Security Council,

Reaffirming its resolutions 1269 (1999) of 19 October 1999 and 1368 (2001) of 12 September 2001,

Reaffirming also its unequivocal condemnation of the terrorist attacks which took place in New York, Washington, District of Columbia and Pennsylvania on 11 September 2001 and expressing its determination to prevent all such acts,

Reaffirming further that such acts, like any act of international terrorism, constitute a threat to international peace and security,

Reaffirming the inherent right of individual or collective self-defense as recognized by the Charter of the United Nations as reiterated in resolution 1368 (2001),

Reaffirming the need to combat by all means, in accordance with the Charter of the United Nations, threats to international peace and security caused by terrorist acts,

Deeply concerned by the increase, in various regions of the world, of acts of terrorism motivated by intolerance or extremism,

Calling on states to work together urgently to prevent and suppress terrorist acts, including through increased cooperation and full implementation of the relevant international conventions relating to terrorism,

Recognizing the need for states to complement international co-operation by taking additional measures to prevent and suppress, in their territories through all lawful means, the financing and preparation of any acts of terrorism,

Reaffirming the principle established by the General Assembly in its declaration of October 1970 (resolution 2625 (XXV)) and reiterated by the Security Council in its resolution 1189 (1998) of 13 August 1998, namely that every state has the duty to refrain from organizing, instigating, assisting, or participating in terrorist acts in another state or acquiescing in organized activities within its territory directed towards the commission of such acts,

Acting under Chapter VII of the Charter of the United Nations,

1. Decides that all states shall:

(a) Prevent and suppress the financing of terrorist acts;

(b) Criminalize the willful provision or collection, by any means, directly or indirectly, of funds by their nationals or in their territories with the intention that the funds should be used, or in the knowledge that they are to be used, in order to carry out terrorist acts;

(c) Freeze without delay funds and other financial assets or eco-nomic resources of persons who commit, or attempt to commit, terrorist acts or participate in or facilitate the commission of ter-rorist acts; of entities owned or controlled directly or indirectly by such persons; and of persons and entities acting on behalf of, or at the direction of such persons and entities, including funds de-rived or generated from property owned or controlled directly or indirectly by such persons and associated persons and entities;

(d) Prohibit their nationals or any persons and entities within their territories from making any funds, financial assets, economic or financial resources, or other related services available, directly or indirectly, for the benefit of persons who commit or attempt to commit, facilitate, or participate in the commission of terrorist acts, of entities owned or controlled, directly or indirectly, by such persons and of persons and entities acting on behalf of or at the direction of such persons;

2. Decides also that all states shall:

(a) Refrain from providing any form of support, active or passive, to entities or persons involved in terrorist acts, including by sup-pressing recruitment of members of terrorist groups and elimi-nating the supply of weapons to terrorists.
(b) Take the necessary steps to prevent the commission of ter-rorist acts, including by provision of early warning to other states by exchange of information.

(c) Deny safe haven to those who finance, plan, support, commit terrorist acts, or provide safe havens;

(d) Prevent those who finance, plan, facilitate, or commit ter-rorist acts from using their respective territories for those pur-poses against other states or their citizens;

(e) Ensure that any person who participates in the financing, planning, preparation or perpetration of terrorist acts, or in sup-porting terrorist acts is brought to justice, and ensure that, in addition to any other measures against them, such terrorist acts are established as serious criminal offences in domestic laws and regulations, and that the punishment duly reflects the seriousness of such terrorist acts;

(f) Afford one another the greatest measure of assistance in connection with criminal investigations or criminal proceedings relating to the financing or support of terrorist acts, including assistance in obtaining evidence in their possession necessary for the proceedings

(g) Prevent the movement of terrorists or terrorist groups by effective border controls and controls on issuance of identity papers and travel documents and through measures for preventing counterfeiting, forgery, or fraudulent use of identity papers and travel documents.

3. Calls upon all states to:

(a) Find ways of intensifying and accelerating the exchange of operational information, especially regarding actions or movements of terrorist persons or networks, forged or falsified travel documents, traffic in arms, explosives, or sensitive materials, use of communications technologies by terrorist groups, and the threat posed by the possession of weapons of mass destruction by terrorist groups;

(b) Exchange information in accordance with international and domestic law and cooperate on administrative and judicial matters to prevent the commission of terrorist acts;

(c) Cooperate, particularly through bilateral and multilateral arrangements and agreements, to prevent and suppress terrorist attacks and take action against perpetrators of such acts;

(d) Become parties as soon as possible to relevant international conventions and protocols relating to terrorism, including the

International Convention for the Suppression of the Financing of Terrorism of 9 December 1999;

(e) Increase cooperation and fully implement the relevant international conventions and protocols relating to terrorism and Security Council resolutions 1269 (1999) and 1368 (2001).

(f) Take appropriate measures in conformity with the relevant provisions of national and international law, including international standards of human rights, before granting refugee status, for the purpose of ensuring that the asylum-seeker has not planned, facilitated, or participated in the commission of terrorist acts;

(g) Ensure, in conformity with international law, that refugee status is not abused by the perpetrators, organizers, or facilitators of terrorist acts, and that claims of political motivation are not recognized as grounds for refusing requests for the extradition of alleged terrorists;

4. Notes with concern the close connection between international terrorism and transnational organized crime, illicit drugs, money laundering, illegal arms trafficking, and illegal movement of nuclear, chemical, biological, and other potentially deadly materials, and in this regard emphasizes the need to enhance coordination of efforts on national, sub-regional, regional, and international levels in order to strengthen a global response to this serious challenge and threat to international security;

5. Declares that acts, methods, and practices of terrorism are contrary to the purposes and principles of the United Nations, and that knowingly financing, planning, and inciting terrorist acts are also contrary to the purposes and principles of the United Nations;

6. Decides to establish, in accordance with rule twenty-eight of its provisional rules of procedure, a committee of the Security Council, consisting of all the members of the Council, to mon-

itor implementation of this resolution with the assistance of appropriate expertise and calls upon all states to report to the committee, no later than ninety days from the date of adoption of this resolution and thereafter according to a timetable to be proposed by the committee, on the steps they have taken to implement this resolution;

7. Directs the committee to delineate its tasks, submit a work program within thirty days of the adoption of this resolution, and to consider the support it requires in consultation with the Secretary-General;

8. Expresses its determination to take all necessary steps in order to ensure the full implementation of this resolution in accordance with its responsibilities under the charter;

9. Decides to remain seized of this matter.

Resolution 1390 (2002), adopted by the Security Council at its 4452nd meeting on 16 January 2002

The Security Council,

Recalling its resolutions 1267 (1999) of 15 October 1999, 1333 (2000) of 19 December 2000, and 1363 (2001) of 30 July 2001;

Reaffirming its previous resolutions on Afghanistan, in particular resolutions 1378 (2001) of 14 November 2001 and 1383 (2001) of 6 December 2001;

Reaffirming also its resolutions 1368 (2001) of 12 September 2001 and 1373 (2001) of 28 September 2001, and reiterating its support for international efforts to root out terrorism, in accordance with the Charter of the United Nations;

Reaffirming its unequivocal condemnation of the terrorist attacks which took place in New York, Washington, and Pennsylvania on 11 September 2001, expressing its determination to prevent all such acts, noting the continued activities of Usama bin Laden and the Al-Qaida network in supporting international terrorism, and expressing its determination to root out this network;

Noting the indictments of Usama bin Laden and his associates by the United States of America for, inter alia, the 7 August 1998 bombings of the United States embassies in Nairobi, Kenya, and Dar es Salaam, Tanzania;
Determining that the Taliban have failed to respond to the demands in paragraph thirteen of resolution 1214 (1998) of 8 December 1998, paragraph two of resolution 1267 (1999), and paragraphs one, two, and three of resolution 1333 (2000);

Condemning the Taliban for allowing Afghanistan to be used as a base for terrorists training and activities, including the export of terrorism by the Al-Qaida network and other terrorist groups, as well as for using foreign mercenaries in hostile actions in the territory of Afghanistan;

Condemning the Al-Qaida network and other associated terrorist groups, for the multiple criminal, terrorist acts, aimed at causing the deaths of numerous innocent civilians, and the destruction of property;

Reaffirming further that acts of international terrorism constitute a threat to international peace and security;

Acting under Chapter VII of the Charter of the United Nations:

1. Decides to continue the measures imposed by paragraph eight (c) of resolution 1333 (2000) and takes note of the continued application of the measures imposed by paragraph four (b) of resolution 1267 (1999), in accordance with paragraph two below and decides to terminate the measures imposed in paragraph 4 (a) of resolution 1267 (1999);

2. Decides that all states shall take the following measures with respect to Usama bin Laden, members of the Al-Qaida organization, the Taliban, and other individuals, groups, undertakings, and entities associated with them, as referred to in the list created pursuant to resolutions 1267 (1999) and 1333 (2000) to be updated regularly by the committee established pursuant to resolution 1267 (1999), hereinafter referred to as the Committee;

(a) Freeze without delay the funds and other financial assets or economic resources of these individuals, groups, undertakings, and entities, including funds derived from property owned or controlled, directly or indirectly, by them or by persons acting on their behalf or at their direction, and ensure that neither these nor any other funds, financial assets, or economic resources are made available, directly or indirectly, for such persons' benefit, by their nationals, or by any persons within their territory;

(b) Prevent the entry into or the transit through their territories of these individuals, provided that nothing in this paragraph shall oblige any state to deny entry into or require the departure from its territories of its own nationals, and this paragraph shall not apply where entry or transit is necessary for the fulfillment of a judicial process or the Committee determines on a case-by-case basis only that entry or transit is justified;

(c) Prevent the direct or indirect supply, sale and transfer, to these individuals, groups, undertakings, and entities from their territories or by their nationals outside their territories, or using their flag vessels or aircraft, of arms and related materiel of all types including weapons and ammunition, military vehicles and equipment, paramilitary equipment, and spare parts for the aforementioned, and technical advice, assistance, or training related to military activities;

3. Decides that the measures referred to in paragraphs one and two above will be reviewed in twelve months, and that at the end of this period, the Council will either allow these measures to continue or decide to improve them, in keeping with the principles and purposes of this resolution;

4. Recalls the obligation placed upon all member states to implement in full resolution 1373 (2001), including with regard to any member of the Taliban, the Al-Qaida organization, and any individuals, groups, undertakings, and entities associated with the Taliban and the Al-Qaida organization, who have participated in the financing, planning, facilitating, preparation, or perpetration of terrorist acts or in supporting terrorist acts;

5. Requests the Committee to undertake the following tasks and to report on its work to the Council with its observations and recommendations;

(a) to update regularly the list referred to in paragraph two above, on the basis of relevant information provided by member states and regional organizations;

(b) to seek from all states information regarding the action taken by them to implement effectively the measures referred to in paragraph two above, and thereafter to request from them whatever further information the Committee may consider necessary;

(c) to make periodic reports to the Council on information submitted to the committee regarding the implementation of this resolution;

(d) to promulgate expeditiously such guidelines and criteria as may be necessary to facilitate the implementation of the measures referred to in paragraph two above;

(e) to make information it considers relevant, including the list referred to in paragraph two above, publicly available through appropriate media;

(f) to cooperate with other relevant Security Council Sanctions Committees and with the Committee established pursuant to paragraph 6 of its resolution 1373 (2001);

6. Requests all states to report to the Committee, no later than ninety days from the date of adoption of this resolution and thereafter according to a timetable to be proposed by the Committee, on the steps they have taken to implement the measures referred to in paragraph two above;

7. Urges all states, relevant United Nations bodies, and, as appropriate, other organizations and interested parties to cooperate fully with the Committee and with the monitoring group referred to in paragraph nine below;

8. Urges all states to take immediate steps to enforce and strengthen through legislative enactments or administrative measures, when appropriate, the measures imposed under domestic laws or regulations against their nationals and other individuals or entities operating on their territories, to prevent and punish violations of the measures referred to in paragraph two of this resolution, to inform the Committee of the adoption of such measures, and invites states to report the results of all related investigations or enforcement actions to the Committee unless to do so would compromise the investigation or enforcement actions;

9. Requests the Secretary-General to assign the monitoring group established pursuant to paragraph four (a) of resolution 1363 (2001), whose mandate expires on 19 January 2002, to monitor, for a period of 1 twelve months, the implementation of the measures referred to in paragraph two of this resolution;

10. Requests the monitoring group to report to the committee by 31 March 2002 and thereafter every four months;

11. Decides to remain actively seized of the matter.

United Nations Convention against Illicit Traffic in Narcotic Drugs and Psychotropic Substances, 1988

Final Act of the United Nations Conference for the Adoption of a Convention against Illicit Traffic in Narcotic Drugs and Psychotropic Substances

1. The General Assembly of the United Nations, by its resolution 39/141 of 14 December 1984, requested the Economic and Social Council of the United Nations, "taking into consideration Article 62, paragraph 3, and Article 66, paragraph 1, of the Charter of the
United Nations and Council resolution 9 (1) of 16 February 1946, to request the Commission on Narcotic Drugs to initiate at its thirty-first session, to be held in February 1985, as a matter of priority, the preparation of a draft Convention against illicit traffic in narcotic drugs which considers the various aspects of the problem as a whole and, in particular, those not envisaged in existing international instruments."

2. In furtherance of the foregoing request and the follow-up action by the Commission on Narcotic Drugs and the Economic and Social Council, the Secretary-General of the United Nations prepared the initial text of a draft Convention against Illicit Traffic in Narcotic Drugs and Psychotropic Substances. On the basis of the comments made thereon by governments and the deliberations of the Commission on Narcotic Drugs on that draft at its thirty-second session in 1987, the Secretary-General prepared a consolidated working document which was circulated to all governments in April 1987 and was considered at two sessions of an open-ended intergovernmental expert group. On 7 December 1987, the General Assembly adopted resolution 42/111, which gave further instructions for advancing the preparation of the draft Convention. As the time available to the expert group had not permitted thorough consideration of all the articles, the General Assembly requested the Secretary-General to consider convening a further intergovernmental expert group, meeting for two weeks immediately prior to the tenth special session of the

Commission on Narcotic Drugs in February 1988, to continue the revision of the working document on the draft Convention against Illicit Traffic in Narcotic Drugs and Psychotropic Substances and, if possible, to reach agreement on the Convention. At its tenth special session held at Vienna from 8 to 19 February 1988, the Commission on Narcotic Drugs reviewed the text of the draft Convention and decided that certain articles thereof should be referred to the Conference to be convened to adopt a Convention. The Commission also recommended certain means to the Economic and Social Council to further the preparation of the draft Convention.

3. The Economic and Social Council, by its resolution 1988/8 of 25 May 1988, having recalled the preparatory work undertaken pursuant to General Assembly resolution 39/141 by the competent United Nations organs, decided "to convene, in accordance with Article 62, paragraph 4, of the Charter of the United Nations and within the provisions of General Assembly resolution 366 (IV) of 3 December 1949, a conference of plenipotentiaries for the adoption of a Convention against Illicit Traffic in Narcotic Drugs and Psychotropic Substances."

By its decision 1988/120, also adopted on 25 May 1988, the Council decided that the Conference should be held at Vienna from 25 November to 20 December 1988, and that the Secretary-General should send invitations to participate in the Conference to those who had been invited to participate in the International Conference on Drug Abuse and Illicit Trafficking, held at Vienna from 17 to 26 June 1987.

4. By its resolution 1988/8, the Economic and Social Council also decided to convene a review group for the Conference to review the draft texts of certain articles and the draft Convention as a whole to achieve overall consistency in the text to be submitted to the Conference. The review group on the draft Convention met at the United Nations Office at Vienna from 27 June to 8 July 1988 and adopted a report to the Conference (E/CONF.82/3).

5. The United Nations Conference for the Adoption of a Convention against Illicit Traffic in Narcotic Drugs and Psychotropic Substances met at the Neue Hofburg at Vienna from 25 November to 20 December 1988.

6. Pursuant to Economic and Social Council resolution 1988/8 of 25 May 1988 and its decision 1988/120 of the same date, the Secretary-General invited to the Conference:

a) All states:

(b) Namibia, represented by the United Nations Council for Namibia;

(c) Representatives of organizations that have received a standing invitation from the General Assembly to participate in the sessions, and the work of all international conferences convened under its auspices in the capacity of observers to participate in the Conference in that capacity, in accordance with Assembly resolutions 3237 (XXIX) of 22 November 1974 and 31/152 of 20 December 1976;
(d) Representatives of the national liberation movements recognized in its region by the Organization of African Unity to participate in the Conference in the capacity of observers, in accordance with General Assembly resolution 3280 (XXIX) of 10 December 1974;

(e) The specialized agencies and the International Atomic Energy Agency, as well as interested organs of the United Nations, to be represented at the Conference;

(f) Other interested intergovernmental organizations to be represented by observers at the Conference;

(g) Interested non-governmental organizations in consultative status with the Economic and Social Council and other interested non-governmental organizations that may have a specific contribution to make to the work of the Conference to be represented by observers at the Conference.

7. The delegations of the following 106 states participated in the Conference: Afghanistan, Albania, Algeria, Argentina, Australia, Austria, Bahamas, Bahrain, Bangladesh, Barbados, Belgium, Bolivia, Botswana, Brazil, Bulgaria, Burma, Byelorussian Soviet Socialist Republic, Cameroon, Canada, Cape Verde, Chile, China, Colombia, Costa Rica, Côte d'lvoire, Cuba, Cyprus, Czechoslovakia, Denmark, Dominican Republic, Ecuador, Egypt, Ethiopia, Finland, France, German Democratic Republic, Germany, Federal Republic of Ghana, Greece, Guatemala, Guinea, Holy See, Honduras, Hungary, India, Indonesia, Iran (Islamic Republic of), Iraq, Ireland, Israel, Italy, Jamaica, Japan, Jordan, Kenya, Kuwait, Libyan Arab Jamahiriya, Luxembourg, Madagascar, Malaysia, Malta, Mauritania, Mauritius, Mexico, Monaco, Morocco, Nepal, Netherlands, New Zealand, Nicaragua, Nigeria, Norway, Oman, Pakistan, Panama, Papua New Guinea, Paraguay, Peru, Philippines, Poland, Portugal, Qatar, Republic of Korea, Saudi Arabia, Senegal, Spain, Sri Lanka, Sudan, Suriname, Sweden, Switzerland, Thailand, Tunisia, Turkey, Ukrainian Soviet Socialist Republic, Union of Soviet Socialist Republics, United Arab Emirates, United Kingdom of Great Britain and Northern Ireland, United Republic of Tanzania, United States of America, Uruguay, Venezuela, Viet Nam, Yemen, Yugoslavia, and Zaire.

8. The representatives of the following national liberation movements, invited to the Conference by the Secretary-General, attended and participated as provided for in the rules of procedure of the Conference (E/CONF.8217): Pan Africanist Congress of Azania and South West Africa People's Organization.

9. The representatives of the following specialized agencies invited to the conference by the Secretary-General attended and participated as provided for in the rules of procedure of the conference: International Civil Aviation Organization, International Labor Organization, United Nations Educational, Scientific and

Cultural Organization, United Nations Industrial Development Organization, and World Health Organization.

10. The representatives of the following other intergovernmental organizations, invited to the Conference by the Secretary-General, attended and participated as provided for in the rules of procedure of the Conference: Arab Security Studies and Training Center, Colombo Plan Bureau, Council of Europe, Customs Co-operation Council, European Economic Community, International Criminal Police Organization, League of Arab States, and South American Agreement on Narcotic Drugs and Psychotropic Substances.

11. The representatives of the following interested United Nations organs and related bodies invited to the Conference by the Secretary-General, attended and participated as provided for in the rules of procedure of the Conference: Centre for Social Development and Humanitarian Affairs, International Narcotics Control Board, United Nations Asia and Far East Institute for the Prevention of Crime and the Treatment of Offenders, and United Nations Fund for Drug Abuse Control.

12. Observers from the following non-governmental organizations, invited to the Conference by the Secretary-General, attended and participated as provided for in the rules of procedure of the Conference: Baha'i International Community, Caritas Internationalis, Centro Italiano de Solidarità, Colombia Therapeutic Communities, Co-ordinating Board of Jewish Organizations, Cruz Blanca Panama, Drug Abuse Prevention Programme, European Union of Women, Integrative Drogenhilfe a.d. Fachhochschule Ffm. e.v., International Abolitionist Federation, International Advertising Association, International Air Transport Association, International Association of Democratic Jurists, International Association of Lions Clubs, International Catholic Child Bureau, International Chamber of Commerce, International Confederation of Free Trade Unions, International Council on Women, International Council of Alcohol and Addictions, International Federation of

Business and Professional Women, International Federation of Social Workers, International Pharmaceutical Federation, International Schools Association, Islamic African Relief Agency, Opium De-addiction Treatment, Training and
Research Trust, Pace United Kingdom International Affairs, Pax Romana, Soroptimist International, World Association of Girl Guides and Girl Scouts, World Union of Catholic Women's Organizations, and Zonta International Committee.

13. The Conference elected Mr. Guillermo Bedregal Gutiérrez (Bolivia) as president.

14. The Conference elected as vice presidents the representatives of the following states:

Algeria, Argentina, Bahamas, China, Côte d'lvoire, France, Iran (Islamic Republic of), Japan, Kenya, Malaysia, Mexico, Morocco, Nigeria, Pakistan, Philippines, Senegal, Sudan, Sweden, Turkey, Union of Soviet Socialist Republics, United Kingdom of Great Britain and Northern Ireland, United States of America, Venezuela, and Yugoslavia.

15. The Conference elected Mrs. Mervat Tallawy (Egypt) as Rapporteur-General.

16. The following committees were set up by the Conference:

General Committee
Chairman: the president of the Conference
Members: the president and vice presidents of the Conference, the
Rapporteur-General of the Conference, the chairmen of the Committees of the Whole and the chairman of the drafting committee
Committees of the Whole:
Committee I
Chairman: Mr. Gioacchino Polimeni (Italy)
Vice chairman: Mr. M.A. Hena (Bangladesh)

Rapporteur: Mr. Oskar Hugler (German Democratic Republic)
Committee II
Chairman: Mr. István Bayer (Hungary)
Vice chairman: Mr. L.H.J.B. van Gorkom (Netherlands)
Rapporteur: Mrs. Yolanda Fernández Ochoa (Costa Rica)

Drafting Committee

Chairman: Mr. M.V.N. Rao (India)
Vice chairman: Mr. Hashem M. Kuraa (Egypt)
Members: the chairman of the drafting committee and the representatives of the following states: Australia, Botswana, Canada, China, Colombia, Czechoslovakia, Egypt, France, Ghana, Iraq, Peru, Senegal, Spain, and Union of Soviet Socialist Republics. The rapporteurs of the Committees of the Whole participated ex officio in the
work of the drafting committee in accordance with rule forty-nine of the rules of procedure of the conference.

Credentials Committee
Chairman: Mr. Edouard Molitor (Luxembourg)
Members: the representatives of the following states: Bolivia, Botswana, China, Côte d'Ivoire, Jamaica, Luxembourg, Thailand, Union of Soviet Socialist Republics, and United States of America.

17. The Secretary-General of the United Nations who was also the Under-Secretary-General and Director-general of the United Nations Office at Vienna was represented by Miss Margaret J. Anstee. Meanwhile, Mr. Francisco Ramos-Galino, director of the Division of Narcotic Drugs, was appointed by the Secretary-General as Executive Secretary.

18. The Conference had before it the report of the review group convened pursuant to Economic and Social Council resolution 1988/8 of 25 May 1988 (E/CONF.82/3). In addition to an account of the work of the review group, the report contained proposals submitted to the review group relating to the draft

Convention for consideration by the Conference, and the text of the draft Convention against Illicit Traffic in Narcotic Drugs and Psychotropic Substances (annex II). This draft Convention constituted the basic proposal for consideration by the Conference.

19. The Conference in the course of its work divided the articles contained in the draft Convention between the two Committees of the Whole (Committee I and Committee 11). Articles one to five and the preamble were referred to Committee 1 and the remaining articles to Committee II. The Committees of the Whole, after agreeing upon the text of a particular article, referred it to the Drafting Committee. The Committees of the Whole reported to the Conference on the outcome of their work, and the Drafting Committee submitted to the Conference a complete text of the draft Convention against Illicit Traffic in Narcotic Drugs and Psychotropic Substances (E/CONF.82/13).

20. On the basis of the deliberations set forth in the records of the conference (E/CONF.82/SR.1 to 8), the Committees of the Whole (E/CONF.82/C.1/SR.1 to 33 and E/CONF.82/C.2/SR.1 to 34), the reports of the Committees of the Whole (E/CONF.82/11and E/CONF.82/12), and the Drafting Committee (E/CONF.82/13), the Conference drew up the following Convention:

United Nations Convention against Illicit Traffic in Narcotic Drugs and Psychotropic Substances

21. The foregoing Convention, which is subject to ratification, acceptance, approval or act of formal confirmation, and which shall remain open for accession, was adopted by the Conference on 19 December 1988 and opened for signature on 20 December 1988, in accordance with its provisions, until 28 February 1989 at the United Nations Office at Vienna and, subsequently, until 20 December 1989, at the Headquarters of the United Nations in New York, the Secretary-General of the United Nations being the depositary.

22. The Conference also adopted the following resolutions, which are annexed to this Final Act:
- Exchange of information
- Provisional application of the United Nations Convention against Illicit Traffic in Narcotic Drugs and Psychotropic Substances
- Provision of necessary resources to the Division of Narcotic Drugs and the secretariat of the International Narcotics Control Board to enable them to discharge the tasks entrusted to them under the International Drug Control Treaties

In witness whereof, the representatives have signed this Final Act. Done at Vienna, this twentieth day of December one thousand nine hundred and eighty eight, in a single copy, which will be deposited to the Secretary-General of the United Nations, in the Arabic, Chinese, English, French, Russian, and Spanish languages, each text being equally authentic.

Resolutions adopted by the United Nations Conference for the adoption of a Convention against Illicit Traffic in Narcotic Drugs and Psychotropic Substances

Resolution One:

Exchange of Information

The United Nations Conference for the Adoption of a Convention against Illicit Traffic in Narcotic Drugs and Psychotropic Substances,

Calling attention to resolution III adopted by the 1961 United Nations Conference for the Adoption of a Single Convention on Narcotic Drugs, in which attention was drawn to the importance of the technical records on international drug traffickers of the International Criminal Police Organization and their use by that organization for the circulation of descriptions of such traffickers,

Considering the machinery developed by the International Criminal Police Organization for the timely and efficient exchange of crime investigation information between police authorities on a worldwide basis,

Recommends that the widest possible use should be made by police authorities of the records and communications system of the International Criminal Police Organization in achieving the goals of the United Nations Convention against Illicit Traffic in Narcotic Drugs and Psychotropic Substances.

Resolution Two

Provisional application of the United Nations Convention against Illicit Traffic in Narcotic Drugs and Psychotropic Substances

The United Nations Conference for the Adoption of a Convention against Illicit Traffic in Narcotic Drugs and Psychotropic Substances:

1. Urges states, to the extent that they are able to do so, to accelerate steps to ratify the United Nations Convention against Illicit Traffic in Narcotic Drugs and Psychotropic Substances so that it enters into force as quickly as possible;
2. Invites states, to the extent that they are able to do so, to apply provisionally the measures provided in the Convention, pending its entry into force for each of them;
3. Requests the Secretary-General to transmit the present resolution to the Economic and Social Council and the General Assembly.

Resolution Three

Provision of necessary resources to the Division of Narcotic Drugs and the secretariat of the International Narcotics Control Board to enable them to discharge the tasks entrusted to them under the International Drug Control Treaties

The United Nations Conference for the Adoption of a Convention against Illicit Traffic in Narcotic Drugs and Psychotropic Substances,

Recognizing that the Single Convention on Narcotic Drugs 1961, that Convention as amended by the 1972 Protocol Amending the Single Convention on Narcotic Drugs, 1961, and the Convention on Psychotropic Substances 1971, remain the basis for international efforts in the control of narcotic drugs and psychotropic substances, and that strict implementation both by governments and by the international control organs of the United Nations of the obligations arising from the conventions is essential to achieve their aims,

Considering that the United Nations Convention against Illicit Traffic in Narcotic Drugs and Psychotropic Substances will create further obligations and financial outlays for governments, the Commission on Narcotic Drugs, the International Narcotics Control Board, and their secretariats,

Deeply disturbed by the impact of recent staffing and budgetary reductions on the capacity of both the Division of Narcotic Drugs and the secretariat of the International Narcotics Control Board to carry out fully their mandated program of work,

1. Urges all member states to take appropriate steps in the General Assembly, as well as in the financial organs of the Assembly to assign the appropriate priority and approve the necessary budgetary appropriations with a view to providing the Division of Narcotic Drugs and the secretariat of the International Narcotics Control Board with the necessary resources to discharge fully the tasks entrusted to them under the United Nations Convention against Illicit Traffic in Narcotic Drugs and Psychotropic Substances, the Single Convention on Narcotic Drugs, 1961, that Convention as amended by the 1972 Protocol Amending the Single Convention on Narcotic Drugs,

1961, and the Convention on Psychotropic Substances, 1971;

2. Requests the Secretary-General to take the necessary steps, within his competence, to give effect to the provisions of paragraph one above.

United Nations Convention against Illicit Traffic in Narcotic Drugs and Psychotropic Substances

The parties to this Convention,

Deeply concerned by the magnitude of and rising trend in the illicit production of, demand for, and traffic in narcotic drugs and psychotropic substances, which pose a serious threat to the health and welfare of human beings and adversely affect the economic, cultural, and political foundations of society,

Deeply concerned also by the steadily increasing inroads into various social groups made by illicit traffic in narcotic drugs and psychotropic substances, and particularly by the fact that children are used in many parts of the world as illicit drug consumers market and for purposes of illicit production, distribution, and trade in narcotic drugs and psychotropic substances, which entails a danger of incalculable gravity,

Recognizing the links between illicit traffic and other related organized criminal activities which undermine the legitimate economies and threaten the stability, security, and sovereignty of states,

Recognizing also that illicit traffic is an international criminal activity, the suppression of which demands urgent attention and the highest priority,

Aware that illicit traffic generates large financial profits and wealth enabling transnational criminal organizations to penetrate, contaminate, and corrupt the structures of government, legitimate commercial and financial business, and society at all its levels,

Determined to deprive persons engaged in illicit traffic of the proceeds of their criminal activities and thereby eliminate their main incentive for so doing,

Desiring to eliminate the root causes of the problem of abuse of narcotic drugs and psychotropic substances, including the illicit demand for such drugs and substances and the enormous profits derived from illicit traffic,

Considering that measures are necessary to monitor certain substances, including precursors, chemicals, and solvents, which are used in the manufacture of narcotic drugs and psychotropic substances, the availability of which has led to an increase in the clandestine manufacture of such drugs and substances,

Determined to improve international co-operation in the suppression of illicit traffic by sea,

Recognizing that eradication of illicit traffic is a collective responsibility of all states and that, to that end, coordinated action within the framework of international co-operation is necessary,

Acknowledging the competence of the United Nations in the field of control of narcotic drugs and psychotropic substances and desirous that the international organs concerned with such control should be within the framework of that organization,

Reaffirming the guiding principles of existing treaties in the field of narcotic drugs and psychotropic substances and the system of control which they embody,

Recognizing the need to reinforce and supplement the measures provided in the Single Convention on Narcotic Drugs, 1961, that Convention as amended by the 1972 Protocol Amending the Single

Convention on Narcotic Drugs 1961, and the 1971 Convention on Psychotropic Substances, in order to counter the magnitude and extent of illicit traffic and its grave consequences,

Recognizing also the importance of strengthening and enhancing effective legal means for international co-operation in criminal matters for suppressing the international criminal activities of illicit traffic,

Desiring to conclude a comprehensive, effective and operative international convention that is directed specifically against illicit traffic and that considers the various aspects of the problem as a whole, in particular those aspects not envisaged in the existing treaties in the field of narcotic drugs and psychotropic substances,

Hereby agree as follows:

Article One

Definitions

Except where otherwise expressly indicated or where the context otherwise requires, the following definitions shall apply throughout this Convention:

a) "Board" means the International Narcotics Control Board established by the Single Convention on Narcotic Drugs, 1961, and that Convention as amended by the 1972 Protocol Amending the Single Convention on Narcotic Drugs, 1961;

b) "Cannabis plant" means any plant of the genus Cannabis;

c) "Coca bush" means the plant of any species of the genus Erythroxylon;

d) "Commercial carrier" means any person or any public, private or other entity engaged in transporting persons, goods, or mails for remuneration, hire, or any other benefit;

e) "Commission" means the Commission on Narcotic Drugs of the Economic and Social Council of the United Nations;

f) "Confiscation," which includes forfeiture where applicable, means the permanent deprivation of property by order of a court or other competent authority;

g) "Controlled delivery" means the technique of allowing illicit or suspect consignments of narcotic drugs, psychotropic substances, substances in Table I and Table II annexed to this Convention, or substances substituted for them, to pass out of, through or into the territory of one or more countries, with the knowledge and under the supervision of their competent authorities, with a view to identifying persons involved in the commission of offences established in accordance with article three, paragraph one of the Convention;

h) "1961 Convention" means the Single Convention on Narcotic Drugs, 1961;

i) "1961 Convention as amended" means the Single Convention on Narcotic Drugs, 1961, as amended by the 1972 Protocol Amending the Single Convention on Narcotic Drugs, 1961;

j) "1971 Convention" means the Convention on Psychotropic Substances, 1971;

k) "Council" means the Economic and Social Council of the United Nations;

l) "Freezing" or "seizure" means temporarily prohibiting the transfer, conversion, disposition or movement of property, or temporarily assuming custody or control of property on the basis of an order issued by a court or a competent authority;

m) "Illicit traffic" means the offenses set forth in article three, paragraphs one and two, of this Convention;

n) "Narcotic drug" means any of the substances, natural or synthetic, in Schedules I and II of the Single Convention on Narcotic Drugs, 1961, and that Convention as amended by the 1972 Protocol Amending the Single Convention on Narcotic Drugs, 1961;

o) "Opium poppy" means the plant of the species Papaver somniferum L;

p) "Proceeds" means any property derived from or obtained, directly or indirectly, through the commission of an offense established in accordance with article three, paragraph one;

q) "Property" means assets of every kind, whether corporeal or incorporeal, movable or immovable, tangible or intangible, and legal documents or instruments evidencing title to, or interest in, such assets;

r) "Psychotropic substance" means any substance, natural or synthetic, or any natural material in Schedules I, II, III, and IV of the Convention on Psychotropic Substances 1971;

s) "Secretary-General" means the Secretary-General of the United Nations;

t) "Table I" and "Table II" mean the correspondingly numbered lists of substances annexed to this Convention, as amended from time to time in accordance with article twelve,

u) "Transit State" means a state through the territory of which illicit narcotic drugs, psychotropic substances, and substances in Table I and Table II are being moved, which is neither the place of origin nor the place of ultimate destination thereof.

Article Two

Scope of the convention

1. The purpose of this Convention is to promote co-operation among the parties so that they may address more effectively the various aspects of illicit traffic in narcotic drugs and psychotropic substances having an international dimension. In carrying out their obligations under the Convention, the parties shall take necessary measures, including legislative and administrative measures, in conformity with the fundamental provisions of their respective domestic legislative systems.

2. The parties shall carry out their obligations under this Convention in a manner consistent with the principles of sovereign equality and territorial integrity of states and that of non-intervention in the domestic affairs of other states.

3. A party shall not undertake in the territory of another party the exercise of jurisdiction and performance of functions which are exclusively reserved for the authorities of that other party by its domestic law.

Article Three

Offences and sanctions

1. Each party shall adopt such measures as may be necessary to establish as criminal offences under its domestic law, when committed intentionally:

a) i) The production, manufacture, extraction, preparation, offering, offering for sale, distribution, sale, delivery on any terms whatsoever, brokerage, dispatch, dispatch in transit, transport, importation, or exportation of any narcotic drug or any psychotropic substance contrary to the provisions of the 1961 Convention, the 1961 Convention as amended or the 1971 Convention;

ii) The cultivation of opium poppy, coca bush, or cannabis plant for the purpose of the production of narcotic drugs contrary to the provisions of the 1961 Convention and the 1961 Convention as amended;

iii) The possession or purchase of any narcotic drug or psychotropic substance for the purpose of any of the activities enumerated in i) above;

iv) The manufacture, transport, or distribution of equipment, materials or of substances listed in Table I and Table II, knowing that they are to be used in or for the illicit cultivation, production or manufacture of narcotic drugs or psychotropic substances;

v) The organization, management, or financing of any of the offences enumerated in i), ii), iii) or iv) above; b) i) The conversion or transfer of property, knowing that such property is derived from any offence or offences established in accordance with subparagraph a) of this paragraph, or from an act of participation in such offence or offences, for the purpose of concealing or disguising the illicit origin of the property or of assisting any person who is involved in the commission of such an offence or offences to evade the legal consequences of his actions;

ii) The concealment or disguise of the true nature, source, location, disposition, movement, rights with respect to, or ownership of property, knowing that such property is derived from an offence or offences established in accordance with subparagraph a) of this paragraph or from an act of participation in such an offence or offences;

c) Subject to its constitutional principles and the basic concepts of its legal system:

i) The acquisition, possession, or use of property, knowing, at the time of receipt, that such property was derived from an offence or offences established in accordance with subparagraph a) of this paragraph or from an act of participation in such offence or offences;

ii) The possession of equipment or materials or substances listed in Table I and Table II, knowing that they are being or are to be used in or for the illicit cultivation, production, or

iii) Publicly inciting or inducing others, by any means, to commit any of the offences established in accordance with this article or to use narcotic drugs or psychotropic substances illicitly;

iv) Participation in, association or conspiracy to commit, attempts to commit, and aiding, abetting, facilitating, and counseling the commission of any of the offences established in accordance with this article.

2. Subject to its constitutional principles and the basic concepts of its legal system, each party shall adopt such measures as may be necessary to establish as a criminal offence under its domestic law, when committed intentionally, the possession, purchase, or cultivation of narcotic drugs or psychotropic substances for personal consumption contrary to the provisions of the 1961 Convention, the 1961 Convention as amended, or the 1971 Convention.

3. Knowledge, intent, or purpose required as an element of an offense set forth in paragraph one of this article may be inferred from objective factual circumstances.

a) Each party shall make the commission of the offences established in accordance with paragraph one of this article liable to sanctions which take into account the grave nature of these offences, such as imprisonment or other forms of deprivation of liberty, pecuniary sanctions, and confiscation.

b) The parties may provide, in addition to conviction or punishment, for an offence established in accordance with paragraph one of this article, that the offender shall undergo measures such as treatment, education, aftercare, rehabilitation, or social reintegration.

c) Notwithstanding the preceding subparagraphs, in appropriate cases of a minor nature, the parties may provide, as alternatives to conviction or punishment, measures such as education, rehabilitation, or social reintegration, as well as, when the offender is a drug abuser, treatment and aftercare.

d) The parties may provide, either as an alternative to conviction or punishment, or in addition to conviction or punishment of an offence established in accordance with paragraph two of this article, measures for the treatment, education, aftercare, rehabilitation, or social reintegration of the offender.

5. The parties shall ensure that their courts and other competent authorities having jurisdiction can take into account factual circumstances which make the commission of the offences established in accordance with paragraph one of this article particularly serious, such as:

a) The involvement in the offence of an organized criminal group to which the offender belongs;

b) The involvement of the offender in other international organized criminal activities;

c) The involvement of the offender in other illegal activities facilitated by commission of the offence;

d) The use of violence or arms by the offender;

e) The fact that the offender holds a public office, and that the offence is connected with the office in question;

f) The victimization or use of minors;

g) The fact that the offence is committed in a penal institution or in an educational institution or social service facility or in their immediate vicinity or in other places to which students resort for educational, sports, and social activities;

h) Prior conviction, particularly for similar offences, whether foreign or domestic, to the extent permitted under the domestic law of a party.

6. The parties shall endeavor to ensure that any discretionary legal powers under their domestic law relating to the prosecution of persons for offenses established in accordance with this article are exercised to maximize the effectiveness of law enforcement measures in respect of those offences, and with due regard to the need to deter the commission of such offences.

7. The parties shall ensure that their courts or other competent authorities bear in mind the serious nature of the offences enumerated in paragraph one of this article and the circumstances enumerated in paragraph five of this article

when considering the eventuality of early release or parole of persons convicted of such offences.

8. Each party shall, where appropriate, establish under its domestic law a long statute of limitations period in which to commence proceedings for any offence established in accordance with paragraph one of this article, and a longer period where the alleged offender has evaded the administration of justice.

9. Each party shall take appropriate measures, consistent with its legal system, to ensure that a person charged with or convicted of an offense established in accordance with paragraph one of this article, who is found within its territory, is present at the necessary criminal proceedings.

10. For the purpose of co-operation among the parties under this Convention, including, in particular, co-operation under articles five, six, seven, and nine, offences established in accordance with this article shall not be considered as fiscal offences or as political offences or regarded as politically motivated without prejudice to the constitutional limitations and the fundamental domestic law of the parties.

11. Nothing contained in this article shall affect the principle that the description of the offences to which it refers and of legal defenses thereto is reserved to the domestic law of a party and that such offences shall be prosecuted and punished in conformity with that law.

Article Four

Jurisdiction

1. Each party:

a) Shall take such measures as may be necessary to establish its jurisdiction over the offences it has established in accordance with article three, paragraph one, when:

i) The offence is committed in its territory;
ii) The offence is committed on board a vessel flying its flag or an aircraft which is registered under its laws at the time the offence is committed;

b) May take such measures as may be necessary to establish its jurisdiction over the offences it has established in accordance with article three, paragraph one, when:

i) The offence is committed by one of its nationals or by a person who has his habitual residence in its territory;
ii) The offence is committed on board a vessel concerning which that party has been authorized to take appropriate action pursuant to article seventeen, provided that such jurisdiction shall be exercised only on the basis of agreements or arrangements referred to in paragraphs four and nine of that article;
iii) The offence is one of those established in accordance with article three, paragraph one, subparagraph c) iv), and is committed outside its territory with a view to the commission, within its territory, of an offence established in accordance with article three, paragraph one.

2. Each party:

a) Shall also take such measures as may be necessary to establish its jurisdiction over the offences it has established in accordance with article three, paragraph one, when the alleged offender is present in its territory, and it does not extradite him to another party on the ground:

i) That the offence has been committed in its territory or on board a vessel flying its flag or an aircraft which was registered under its law at the time the offence was committed; or

ii) That the offence has been committed by one of its nationals;

b) May also take such measures as may be necessary to establish its jurisdiction over the offences it has established in accordance with article three, paragraph one, when the alleged offender is present in its territory, and it does not extradite him to another party.

3. This Convention does not exclude the exercise of any criminal jurisdiction established by a party in accordance with its domestic law.

Article Five

Confiscation

1. Each party shall adopt such measures as may be necessary to enable confiscation of:

a) Proceeds derived from offences established in accordance with article three, paragraph one, or property, the value of which corresponds to that of such proceeds;

b) Narcotic drugs and psychotropic substances, materials, and equipment or other instrumentalities used in or intended for use in any manner in offences established in accordance with article three, paragraph one.

2. Each party shall also adopt such measures as may be necessary to enable its competent authorities to identify, trace, and freeze or seize proceeds, property, instrumentalities,

or any other things referred to in paragraph one of this article, for the purpose of eventual confiscation.

3. In order to carry out the measures referred to in this article, each party shall empower its courts or other competent authorities to order that bank, financial or commercial records, be made available or be seized. A party shall not decline to act under the provisions of this paragraph on the ground of bank secrecy over an offence established in accordance with article three, paragraph one, the party in whose territory proceeds, property, instrumentalities, or any other things referred to in paragraph one of this article are situated shall:

   i) Submit the request to its competent authorities for the purpose of obtaining an order of confiscation, and if such order is granted, give effect to it or;

   ii) Submit to its competent authorities, with a view to giving effect to it to the extent requested, an order of confiscation issued by the requesting party in accordance with paragraph one of this article, in so far as it relates to proceeds, property, instrumentalities, or any other things referred to in paragraph one situated in the territory of the requested party.

b) Following a request made pursuant to this article by another party having jurisdiction over an offense established in accordance with article three, paragraph one, the requested party shall take measures to identify, trace, and freeze or seize proceeds, property, instrumentalities, or any other things referred to in paragraph one of this article for the purpose of eventual confiscation to be ordered either by the requesting party or pursuant to a request under subparagraph a) of this paragraph, by the requested party.

c) The decisions or actions provided for in subparagraphs a) and b) of this paragraph shall be taken by the requested party, in accordance with and subject to the provisions of its domestic law and its procedural rules or any bilateral or multilateral treaty, agreement or arrangement, to which it may be bound in relation to the requesting party.

d) The provisions of article seven, paragraphs six to nineteen are applicable mutatis mutandis. In addition to the information specified in article seven, paragraph ten, requests made pursuant to this article shall contain the following:

i) In the case of a request pertaining to subparagraph a) i) of this paragraph, a description of the property to be confiscated and a statement of the facts relied upon by the requesting party sufficient to enable the requested party to seek the order under its domestic law;

ii) In the case of a request pertaining to subparagraph a) ii), a legally admissible copy of an order of confiscation issued by the requesting party upon which the request is based, a statement of the facts and information as to the extent to which the execution of the order is requested;

iii) In the case of a request pertaining to subparagraph b), a statement of the facts relied upon by the requesting party and a description of the actions requested.

e) Each party shall furnish to the Secretary-General the text of any of its laws and regulations which give effect to this paragraph and the text of any subsequent changes to such laws and regulations.

f) If a party elects to make the taking of the measures referred to in subparagraphs a) and b) of this paragraph conditional on the existence of a relevant treaty, that party shall consider this convention as the necessary and sufficient treaty basis.

g) The parties shall seek to conclude bilateral and multilateral treaties, agreements or arrangements, to enhance the effectiveness of international co-operation pursuant to this article.

5. a) Proceeds or property confiscated by a party, pursuant to paragraph one or paragraph four of this article shall be disposed of by that party according to its domestic law and administrative procedures.

b) When acting on the request of another party in accordance with this article, a party may give special consideration to concluding agreements on:

i) Contributing the value of such proceeds and property, or funds derived from the sale of such proceeds or property, or a substantial part thereof to intergovernmental bodies specializing in the fight against illicit traffic in and abuse of narcotic drugs and psychotropic substances;

ii) Sharing with other parties, on a regular or case-by-case basis, such proceeds or property, or funds derived from the sale of such proceeds or property, in accordance with its domestic law, administrative procedures or bilateral or multilateral agreements entered into for this purpose.

6. a) If proceeds have been transformed or converted into other property, such property shall be liable to the measures referred to in this article instead of the proceeds. If proceeds have been intermingled with property acquired from legitimate sources, such property shall, without prejudice to any powers relating to seizure or freezing, be liable to confiscation up to the assessed value of the intermingled proceeds.

c) Income or other benefits derived from:

i) Proceeds;

ii) Property into which proceeds have been transformed or converted or;

iii) Property with which proceeds have been intermingled shall also be liable to the measures referred to in this article, in the same manner and to the same extent as proceeds.

7. Each party may consider ensuring that the onus of proof be reversed regarding the lawful origin of alleged proceeds or other property liable to confiscation, to the extent that such action is consistent with the principles of its domestic law and with the nature of the judicial and other proceedings.

8. The provisions of this article shall not be construed as prejudicing the rights of bona fide third parties.

9. Nothing contained in this article shall affect the principle that the measures to which it refers shall be defined and implemented in accordance with and subject to the provisions of the domestic law of a party.

Article Six

Extradition

1. This article shall apply to the offences established by the parties in accordance with article three, paragraph one.

2. Each of the offences to which this article applies shall be deemed to be included as an extraditable offence in any extradition treaty existing between parties. The parties undertake to include such offences as extraditable offenses in every extradition treaty to be concluded between them.

3. If a party which makes extradition conditional on the existence of a treaty receives a request for extradition from

another party with which it has no extradition treaty, it may consider this convention as the legal basis for extradition in respect of any offence to which this article applies. The parties which require detailed legislation in order to use this Convention as a legal basis for extradition shall consider enacting such legislation as may be necessary.

4. The parties which do not make extradition conditional on the existence of a treaty shall recognize offences to which this article applies as extraditable offences between themselves.

5. Extradition shall be subject to the conditions provided for by the law of the requested party or by applicable extradition treaties, including the grounds upon which the requested party may refuse extradition.

6. In considering requests received pursuant to this article, the requested state may refuse to comply with such requests where there are substantial grounds leading its judicial or other competent authorities to believe that compliance would facilitate the prosecution or punishment of any person on account of his race, religion, nationality, political opinions, or would cause prejudice for any of those reasons to any person affected by the request.

7. The parties shall endeavor to expedite extradition procedures and to simplify evidentiary requirements relating thereto in respect of any offence to which this article applies.

8. Subject to the provisions of its domestic law and its extradition treaties, the requested party may, upon being satisfied that the circumstances so warrant and are urgent, and at the request of the requesting party, take a person whose extradition is sought and who is present in its ter-

ritory into custody or take other appropriate measures to ensure his presence at extradition proceedings.

Without prejudice to the exercise of any criminal jurisdiction established in accordance with its domestic law, a party in whose territory an alleged offender is found shall:

a) If it does not extradite him in respect of an offence established in accordance with article three, paragraph one, on the grounds set forth in article four, paragraph two, sub-paragraph a), submit the case to its competent authorities for the purpose of prosecution, unless otherwise agreed with the requesting party;

b) If it does not extradite him in respect of such an offence and has established its jurisdiction in relation to that offense in accordance with article four, paragraph two sub-paragraph b), submit the case to its competent authorities for the purpose of prosecution, unless otherwise requested by the requesting party for the purposes of preserving its legitimate jurisdiction.

10. If extradition, sought for purposes of enforcing a sentence, is refused because the person sought is a national of the requested party, the requested party shall, if its law so permits and in conformity with the requirements of such law upon application of the requesting party, consider the enforcement of the sentence which has been imposed under the law of the requesting party or the remainder thereof.

11. The parties shall seek to conclude bilateral and multilateral agreements to carry out or to enhance the effectiveness of extradition.

12. The parties may consider entering into bilateral or multilateral agreements, whether ad hoc or general, on the transfer to their country of persons sentenced to imprisonment and other forms of deprivation of liberty for of-

fences to which this article applies, in order that they may complete their sentences there.

Article Seven

Mutual Legal Assistance

1. The parties shall afford one another, pursuant to this article, the widest measure of mutual legal assistance in investigations, prosecutions, and judicial proceedings in relation to criminal offenses established in accordance with article three, paragraph one.

2. Mutual legal assistance to be afforded in accordance with this article may be requested for any of the following purposes:

a) Taking evidence or statements from persons;
b) Effecting service of judicial documents;
c) Executing searches and seizures;
d) Examining objects and sites;
e) Providing information and evidentiary items;
f) Providing originals or certified copies of relevant documents and records, including bank, financial, corporate, or business records;
g) Identifying or tracing proceeds, property, instrumentalities, or other things for evidentiary purposes.

3. The parties may afford one another any other forms of mutual legal assistance allowed by the domestic law of the requested party.

4. Upon request, the parties shall facilitate or encourage, to the extent consistent with their domestic law and practice, the presence or availability of persons, including persons in custody, who consent to assist in investigations or participate in proceedings.

5. A party shall not decline to render mutual legal assistance under this article on the ground of bank secrecy.

6. The provisions of this article shall not affect the obligations under any other treaty, bilateral or multilateral, which governs or will govern, in whole or in part, mutual legal assistance in criminal matters.

7. Paragraphs eight to nineteen of this article shall apply to requests made pursuant to this article if the parties in question are not bound by a treaty of mutual legal assistance. If these parties are bound by such a treaty, the corresponding provisions of that treaty shall apply unless the parties agree to apply paragraphs eight to nineteen of this article in lieu thereof. Parties shall designate an authority, or when necessary, authorities who shall have the responsibility and power to execute requests for mutual legal assistance or to transmit them to the competent authorities for execution. The authority or the authorities designated for this purpose shall be notified to the Secretary-General. Transmission of requests for mutual legal assistance and any communication related thereto shall be effected between the authorities designated by the parties; this requirement shall be without prejudice to the right of a party to require that such requests and communications be addressed to it through the diplomatic channel and, in urgent circumstances, where the parties agree, through channels of the International Criminal Police Organization, if possible.

9. Requests shall be made in writing in a language acceptable to the requested party. The language or languages acceptable to each party shall be notified to the Secretary-General. In urgent circumstances, and where agreed by the parties, requests may be made orally, but shall be confirmed in writing forthwith.

10. A request for mutual legal assistance shall contain:

a) The identity of the authority making the request;

b) The subject matter and nature of the investigation, prosecution or proceeding to which the request relates, and the name and the functions of the authority conducting such investigation, prosecution or proceeding;

c) A summary of the relevant facts, except in respect of requests for the purpose of service of judicial documents;

d) A description of the assistance sought and details of any particular procedure the requesting party wishes to be followed;

e) Where possible, the identity, location, and nationality of any person concerned;

f) The purpose for which the evidence, information, or action is sought.

11. The requested party may request additional information when it appears necessary for the execution of the request in accordance with its domestic law or when it can facilitate such execution.

12. A request shall be executed in accordance with the domestic law of the requested party and, to the extent not contrary to the domestic law of the requested party and where possible, in accordance with the procedures specified in the request.

13. The requesting party shall neither transmit nor use information or evidence furnished by the requested party for investigations, prosecutions, or proceedings other than those stated in the request without the prior consent of the requested party.

14. The requesting party may require that the requested party keep confidential the fact and substance of the request,

except to the extent necessary to execute the request. If the requested party cannot comply with the requirement of confidentiality, it shall promptly inform the requesting party.

15. Mutual legal assistance may be refused:

a) If the request is not made in conformity with the provisions of this article;

b) If the requested party considers that execution of the request is likely to prejudice its sovereignty, security, order public, or other essential interests;

c) If the authorities of the requested party would be prohibited by its domestic law from carrying out the action requested with regard to any similar offence, had it been subject to investigation, prosecution or proceedings under their own jurisdiction;

d) If it would be contrary to the legal system of the requested party relating to mutual legal assistance for the request to be granted;

16. Reasons shall be given for any refusal of mutual legal assistance;

17. Mutual legal assistance may be postponed by the requested party on the ground that it interferes with an ongoing investigation, prosecution, or proceeding. In such a case, the requested party shall consult with the requesting party to determine if the assistance can still be given subject to such terms and conditions as the requested party deems necessary.

18. A witness, expert, or other person who consents to give evidence in a proceeding or to assist in an investigation, prosecution, or judicial proceeding in the territory of the

requesting party shall not be prosecuted, detained, punished, or subjected to any other restriction of his personal liberty in that territory in respect of acts, omissions, or convictions prior to his departure from the territory of the requested party. Such safe conduct shall cease when the witness, expert, or other person having had, for a period of fifteen consecutive days or for any period agreed upon by the parties from the date on which he has been officially informed that his presence is no longer required by the judicial authorities, an opportunity of leaving has nevertheless remained voluntarily in the territory or, having left it, has returned of his own free will.

19. The ordinary costs of executing a request shall be borne by the requested party, unless otherwise agreed by the parties concerned. If expenses of a substantial or extraordinary nature are or will be required to fulfill the request, the parties shall consult to determine the terms and conditions under which the request will be executed, as well as the manner in which the costs shall be borne.

20. The parties shall consider, as may be necessary, the possibility of concluding bilateral or multilateral agreements or arrangements that would serve the purposes of, give practical effect to, or enhance the provisions of this article.

Article Eight

Transfer of Proceedings

The parties shall give consideration to the possibility of transferring to one another proceedings for criminal prosecution of offences established in accordance with article three, paragraph one, in cases where such transfer is considered to be in the interests of a proper administration of justice.

Article Nine

Other forms of cooperation and training

1. The parties shall co-operate closely with one another, consistent with their respective domestic legal and administrative systems, with a view to enhancing the effectiveness of law enforcement action to suppress the commission of offences established in accordance with article three, paragraph one. They shall, in particular, on the basis of bilateral or multilateral agreements or arrangements:

   a) Establish and maintain channels of communication between their competent agencies and services to facilitate the secure and rapid exchange of information concerning all aspects of offences established in accordance with article 3, paragraph 1, including, if the Parties concerned deem it appropriate, links with other criminal activities;

   b) Co-operate with one another in conducting enquiries, with respect to offences established in accordance with article 3, paragraph 1, having an international character, concerning:

   i) The identity, whereabouts, and activities of persons suspected of being involved in offenses established in accordance with article three, paragraph one;

   ii) The movement of proceeds or property derived from the commission of suchoffences;

   iii) The movement of narcotic drugs, psychotropic substances, substances in Table I and Table II of this Convention, and instrumentalities used or intended for use in the commission of such offences;

   c) In appropriate cases and if not contrary to domestic law, establish joint teams, taking into account the need to protect the security of persons and of operations to carry out the provisions of this paragraph. The officials of any party taking part in such teams shall act as authorized by the appropriate authorities of the party in whose territory the operation is to take place; in all such cases, the parties involved shall ensure that the sovereignty of the party on whose territory the operation is to take place is fully respected;

d) Provide, when appropriate, necessary quantities of substances for analytical or investigative purposes;

e) Facilitate effective co-ordination between their competent agencies and services and promote the exchange of personnel and other experts, including the posting of liaison officers. Each party shall, to the extent necessary, initiate, develop, or improve specific training programs for its law enforcement and other personnel, including customs, charged with the suppression of offences established in accordance with article three, paragraph one. Such programs shall deal, in particular, with the following:

a) Methods used in the detection and suppression of offences established in accordance with article three, paragraph one;

b) Routes and techniques used by persons suspected of being involved in offences established in accordance with article three, paragraph one, particularly in transit states, and appropriate countermeasures;

c) Monitoring of the import and export of narcotic drugs, psychotropic substances, and substances in Table I and Table II;

d) Detection and monitoring of the movement of proceeds and property derived from, narcotic drugs, psychotropic substances, substances in Table I and Table II, and instrumentalities used or intended for use in the commission of

offences established in accordance with article three, paragraph one;

e) Methods used for the transfer, concealment, or disguise
   of such proceeds, property, and instrumentalities;

f) Collection of evidence;
g) Control techniques in free trade zones and free ports and;
h) Modern law enforcement techniques.

3. The parties shall assist one another to plan and implement
   research and training programs designed to share expertise
   in the areas referred to in paragraph two of this article and,
   to this end, shall also, when appropriate, use regional and
   international conferences and seminars to promote co-operation and stimulate discussion on problems of mutual
   concern, including the special problems and needs of
   transit states.

Article Ten

International cooperation and assistance for transit states
1. The parties shall co-operate, directly or through competent international or regional organizations, to assist and
   support transit states and, in particular, developing countries in need of such assistance and support, to the extent
   possible, through programs of technical co-operation on
   interdiction and other related activities.

2. The parties may undertake, directly or through competent
   international or regional organizations, to provide financial assistance to such transit states for the purpose of aug-
   menting and strengthening the infrastructure needed for
   effective control and prevention of illicit traffic.

3. The parties may conclude bilateral or multilateral agreements or arrangements to enhance the effectiveness of international co-operation pursuant to this article and may

take into consideration financial arrangements in this regard.

Article Eleven

Controlled delivery

1. If permitted by the basic principles of their respective domestic legal systems, the parties shall take the necessary measures, within their possibilities, to allow for the appropriate use of controlled delivery at the international level on the basis of agreements or arrangements mutually consented to, with a view to identifying persons involved in offences established in accordance with article three, paragraph one and to taking legal action against them.

2. Decisions to use controlled delivery shall be made on a case-by-case basis and may, when necessary, take into consideration financial arrangements and understandings with respect to the exercise of jurisdiction by the parties concerned.

3. Illicit consignments whose controlled delivery is agreed to may, with the consent of the parties concerned, be intercepted and allowed to continue with the narcotic drugs or psychotropic substances intact or removed or replaced in whole or in part.

Article Twelve

Substances frequently used in the illicit manufacture or narcotic drugs or psychotropic substances

1. The parties shall take the measures they deem appropriate to prevent diversion of substances in Table I and Table II used for the purpose of illicit manufacture of narcotic

drugs or psychotropic substances and shall co-operate with one another to this end.

2. If a party or the Board has information which in its opinion may require the inclusion of a substance in Table I or Table II, it shall notify the Secretary-General and furnish him with the information in support of that notification. The procedure described in paragraphs two to seven of this article shall also apply when a party or the Board has information justifying the deletion of a substance from Table I or Table II or the transfer of a substance from one table to the other.

3. The Secretary-General shall transmit such notification and any information which he or she considers relevant to the parties, to the Commission, and where notification is made by a party to the Board. The parties shall communicate their comments concerning the notification to the Secretary-General, together with all supplementary information which may assist the Board in establishing an assessment and the commission in reaching a decision.

4. If the Board, taking into account the extent, importance, and diversity of the licit use of the substance, and the possibility and ease of using alternate substances both for licit purposes and for the illicit manufacture of narcotic drugs or psychotropic substances finds:

a) That the substance is frequently used in the illicit manufacture of a narcotic drug or psychotropic substance;

b) That the volume and extent of the illicit manufacture of a narcotic drug or psychotropic substance creates serious public health or social problems, so as to warrant international action, it shall communicate to the Commission an assessment of the substance, including the likely effect of adding the substance to either Table I or Table II on both licit use and illicit manufacture, together with recommendations of monitoring measures, if any, that would be appropriate in the light of its assessment.

5. The Commission, taking into account the comments submitted by the parties and the comments and recommendations of the Board, whose assessment shall be determinative as to scientific matters and also taking into due consideration any other relevant factors, may decide by a two-thirds majority of its members to place a substance in Table I or Table II.

6. Any decision of the Commission taken pursuant to this article shall be communicated by the Secretary-General to all states and other entities which are, or which are entitled to become, parties to this Convention and to the Board. Such decision shall become fully effective with respect to each party, one hundred and eighty days after the date of such communication.

7. a) The decisions of the Commission taken under this article shall be subject to review by the Council upon the request of any party filed within one hundred and eighty days after the date of notification of the decision. The request for review shall be sent to the Secretary-General, together with all relevant information upon which the request for review is based.

b) The Secretary-General shall transmit copies of the request for review and the relevant information to the Commission, to the Board, and to all the parties, inviting them to submit their comments within ninety days. All comments received shall be submitted to the Council for consideration.

c) The Council may confirm or reverse the decision of the Commission. Notification of the Council's decision shall be transmitted to all states and other entities which are, or which are entitled to become, parties to this Convention, to the Commission, and to the Board.

8. a) Without prejudice to the generality of the provisions contained in paragraph one of this article, the provisions of the 1961 Convention, the 1961 Convention as amended, and the 1971 Convention, the parties shall take the measures they deem appropriate to monitor the manufacture and distribution of substances in Table I and Table II which are carried out within their territory.

To this end, the parties may:

i) Control all persons and enterprises engaged in the manufacture and distribution of such substances;
ii) Control under license the establishment and premises in which such manufacture or distribution may take place;

ii) Require that licensees obtain a permit for conducting the aforesaid operations;

iv) Prevent the accumulation of such substances in the possession of manufacturers and distributors, in excess of the quantities required for the normal conduct of business and the prevailing market conditions.

9. Each party shall, with respect to substances in Table I and Table II, take the following measures:

a) Establish and maintain a system to monitor international trade in substances in Table I and Table II in order to facilitate the identification of suspicious transactions. Such monitoring systems shall be applied in close co-operation with manufacturers, importers, exporters, wholesalers, and retailers who shall inform the competent authorities of suspicious orders and transactions.

b) Provide for the seizure of any substance in Table I or Table II if there is sufficient evidence that it is for use in the illicit manufacture of a narcotic drug or psychotropic substance.

c) Notify, as soon as possible, the competent authorities and services of the parties concerned if there is reason to believe that the import, export, or transit of a substance in Table I or Table II is destined for the illicit manufacture of narcotic drugs or psychotropic substances, including, in particular, information about the means of payment and any other essential elements which led to that belief.

d) Require that imports and exports be properly labeled and documented. Commercial documents such as invoices, cargo manifests, customs, transport, and other shipping documents shall include the names, as stated in Table I or Table II, of the substances being imported or exported, the quantity being imported or exported, and the name and address of the exporter, the importer and, when available, the consignee.

e) Ensure that documents referred to in subparagraph d) of this paragraph are maintained for a period of not less than two years and may be made available for inspection by the competent authorities.

10.a) In addition to the provisions of paragraph nine and upon request to the Secretary-General by the interested party, each Party from whose territory a substance in Table I is to be exported shall ensure that, prior to such export, the following information is supplied by its competent authorities to the competent authorities of the importing country:

i) Name and address of the exporter and importer and, when available, the consignee;

ii) Name of the substance in Table I;

iii) Quantity of the substance to be exported;

iv) Expected point of entry and expected date of dispatch;

v) Any other information which is mutually agreed upon by the parties.

b) A party may adopt more strict or severe measures of control than those provided by this paragraph if, in its opinion, such measures are desirable or necessary.

11. Where a party furnishes information to another party in accordance with paragraphs nine and ten of this article, the party furnishing such information may require that the party receiving it keeps confidential any trade, business, commercial, or professional secret or trade process.

12. Each party shall furnish annually to the Board, in the form and manner provided for by it and on forms made available by it, information on:

a) The amounts seized of substances in Table I and Table II and, when known, their origin;

b) Any substance not included in Table I or Table II which is identified as having been used in illicit manufacture of narcotic drugs or psychotropic substances, and which is deemed by the party to be sufficiently significant to be brought to the attention of the Board and;

c) Methods of diversion and illicit manufacture.

13. The Board shall report annually to the commission on the implementation of this article, and the commission shall periodically review the adequacy and propriety of Table I and Table II.

The provisions of this article shall apply neither to pharmaceutical preparations nor to other preparations containing substances in Table I or Table II that are compounded in such a way that such substances cannot be easily used or recovered by readily applicable means.

Article Thirteen

Materials and equipment

The parties shall take such measures as they deem appropriate to prevent trade in and the diversion of materials and equipment for illicit production or manufacture of narcotic drugs and psychotropic substances shall co-operate to this end.

Article Fourteen

Measures to eradicate illicit cultivation of narcotic plants and to eliminate illicit demand for narcotic drugs and psychotropic substances

1. Any measures taken pursuant to this Convention by parties shall not be less stringent than the provisions applicable to the eradication of illicit cultivation of plants containing narcotic and psychotropic substances and to the elimination of illicit demand for narcotic drugs and psychotropic substances under the provisions of the 1961 Convention, the 1961 Convention as amended, and the 1971 Convention.

2. Each party shall take appropriate measures to prevent illicit cultivation of and to eradicate plants containing narcotic or psychotropic substances, such as opium poppy, coca bush, and cannabis plants, cultivated illicitly in its territory. The measures adopted shall respect fundamental human rights and shall take due account of traditional licit uses, where there is historic evidence of such use, as well as the protection of the environment.

3. a) The parties may co-operate to increase the effectiveness of eradication efforts. Such co-operation may, *inter alia,*

include support, when appropriate, for integrated rural development leading to economically viable alternatives to illicit cultivation. Factors such as access to markets, the availability of resources, and prevailing socioeconomic conditions should be taken into account before such rural development programs are implemented. The parties may agree on any other appropriate measures of co-operation.

b) The parties shall also facilitate the exchange of scientific and technical information and the conduct of research concerning eradication.

c) Whenever they have common frontiers, the parties shall seek to co-operate in eradication programs in their respective areas along those frontiers.

4. The parties shall adopt appropriate measures aimed at eliminating or reducing illicit demand for narcotic drugs and psychotropic substances, with a view to reducing human suffering and eliminating financial incentives for illicit traffic. These measures may be based, *inter alia*, on the recommendations of the United Nations, specialized agencies of the United Nations such as the World Health Organization, and other competent international organizations, and on the Comprehensive Multidisciplinary Outline adopted by the International Conference on Drug Abuse and Illicit Trafficking, held in 1987, as it pertains to governmental and non-governmental agencies and private efforts in the fields of prevention, treatment, and rehabilitation. The parties may enter into bilateral or multilateral agreements or arrangements aimed at eliminating or reducing illicit demand for narcotic drugs and psychotropic substances.

5. The parties may also take necessary measures for early destruction or lawful disposal of the narcotic drugs, psychotropic substances, and substances in Table I and Table II which have been seized or confiscated and for the ad-

missibility as evidence of duly certified necessary quantities of such substances.

Article Fifteen

Commercial carriers

1. The parties shall take appropriate measures to ensure that means of transport operated by commercial carriers are not used in the commission of offences established in accordance with article three, paragraph one; such measures may include special arrangements with commercial carriers.

2. Each party shall require commercial carriers to take reasonable precautions to prevent the use of means of transport for the commission of offences established in accordance with article three, paragraph one. Such precautions may include:

a) If the principal place of business of a commercial carrier is within the territory of the party:

i) Training of personnel to identify suspicious consignments or persons;
ii) Promotion of integrity of personnel;

b) If a commercial carrier is operating within the territory of the party:
i) Submission of cargo manifests in advance, whenever possible;
ii) Use of tamper-resistant, individually verifiable seals on containers;
iii) Reporting to the appropriate authorities at the earliest opportunity all suspicious circumstances that may be related to the commission of offences established in accordance with article three, paragraph one.

3. Each party shall seek to ensure that commercial carriers and the appropriate authorities at points of entry and exit and other customs control areas co-operate, with a view to preventing unauthorized access to means of transport and cargo and to implementing appropriate security measures.

Article Sixteen

Commercial documents and labeling of exports

1. Each party shall require that lawful exports of narcotic drugs and psychotropic substances be properly documented. In addition to the requirements for documentation under article thirty-one of the 1961 Convention, article thirty-one of the 1961 Convention as amended, and article twelve of the 1971 Convention, commercial documents such as invoices, cargo manifests, customs, transport, and other shipping documents shall include the names of the narcotic drugs and psychotropic substances being exported as set out in the respective schedules of the 1961 Convention, the 1961 Convention as amended and the 1971 Convention, the quantity being exported, and the name and address of the exporter, the importer and, when available, the consignee.

2. Each party shall require that consignments of narcotic drugs and psychotropic substances being exported be not mislabeled.

Article Seventeen

Illicit traffic by sea

1. The parties shall co-operate to the fullest extent possible to suppress illicit traffic by sea, in conformity with the international law of the sea.

2. A party which has reasonable grounds to suspect that a vessel flying its flag or not displaying a flag or marks of registry is engaged in illicit traffic may request the assistance of other parties in suppressing its use for that purpose. The parties so requested shall render such assistance within the means available to them.

3. A party which has reasonable grounds to suspect that a vessel exercising freedom of navigation in accordance with international law, flying the flag, or displaying marks of registry of another party, is engaged in illicit traffic may so notify the flag state, request confirmation of registry, and if confirmed, request authorization from the flag state to take appropriate measures in regard to that vessel.

4. In accordance with paragraph three or in accordance with treaties in force between them or in accordance with any agreement or arrangement otherwise reached between those parties, the flag state may authorize the requesting state to *inter aria*:

a) Board the vessel;
b) Search the vessel;
c) If evidence of involvement in illicit traffic is found, take appropriate action with respect to the vessel, persons, and cargo on board. Where action is taken pursuant to this article, the parties concerned shall take due account of the need not to endanger the safety of life at sea, the security of the vessel and the cargo, or to prejudice the commercial and legal interests of the flag state or any other interested state.

6. The flag state may, consistent with its obligations in paragraph one of this article, subject its authorization to conditions to be mutually agreed between it and the requesting party, including conditions relating to responsibility.

7. For the purposes of paragraphs three and four of this article, a party shall respond expeditiously to a request from another party to determine whether a vessel that is flying its flag is entitled to do so and to request for authorization made pursuant to paragraph three. At the time of becoming a party to this convention, each party shall designate an authority or when necessary, authorities to receive and respond to such requests. Such designation shall be notified through the Secretary-General to all other parties within one month of the designation.

8. A party which has taken any action in accordance with this article shall promptly inform the flag state concerned of the results of that action.

9. The parties shall consider entering into bilateral or regional agreements or arrangements to carry out or to enhance the effectiveness of the provisions of this article.

10. Action pursuant to paragraph four of this article shall be carried out only by warships or military aircraft or other ships or aircraft clearly marked and identifiable as being on government service and authorized to that effect.

11. Any action taken in accordance with this article shall take due account of the need not to interfere with or affect the rights, obligations, and the exercise of jurisdiction of coastal states in accordance with the international law of the sea.

Article Eighteen

Free trade zones and free ports

1. The parties shall apply measures to suppress illicit traffic in narcotic drugs, psychotropic substances, and substances in Table I and Table II in free trade zones and in free ports

that are no less stringent than those applied in other parts of their territories.

2. The parties shall endeavor:

a) To monitor the movement of goods and persons in free trade zones and free ports and to that end, shall empower the competent authorities to search cargoes and incoming and outgoing vessels, including pleasure craft and fishing vessels, as well as aircraft and vehicles and when appropriate, to search crew members, passengers, and their baggage;

b) To establish and maintain a system to detect consignments suspected of containing narcotic drugs, psychotropic substances, and substances in Table I and Table II, passing into or out of free trade zones and free ports;

c) To establish and maintain surveillance systems in harbor and dock areas and at airports and border control points in free trade zones and free ports.

Article Nineteen

The use of mails

1. In conformity with their obligations under the Conventions of the Universal Postal Union and in accordance with the basic principles of their domestic legal systems, the parties shall adopt measures to suppress the use of the mails for illicit traffic and shall co-operate with one another to that end.

2. The measures referred to in paragraph one of this article shall include, in particular:

a) Coordinated action for the prevention and repression of the use of the mails for illicit traffic;

b) Introduction and maintenance by authorized law enforcement personnel of investigative and control techniques designed to detect illicit consignments of narcotic drugs, psychotropic substances, and substances in Table I and Table II in the mails and legislative measures to enable the use of appropriate means to secure evidence required for judicial proceedings.

Article Twenty

Information to be furnished by the parties

1. The parties shall furnish, through the Secretary-General, information to the Commission on the working of this Convention in their territories and in particular:

a) The text of laws and regulations promulgated in order to give effect to the Convention; and

b) Particulars of cases of illicit traffic within their jurisdiction which they consider important because of new trends disclosed, the quantities involved, the sources from which the substances are obtained, or the methods employed by persons so engaged.

2. The parties shall furnish such information in such a manner and by such dates as the Commission may request.

Article Twenty-one

Functions of the Commission

The Commission is authorized to consider all matters pertaining to the aims of this Convention and in particular:

a) The Commission shall, on the basis of the information submitted by the parties in accordance with article twenty, review the operation of this Convention;

b) The Commission may make suggestions and general recommendations based on the examination of the information received from the parties;

c) The Commission may call the attention of the Board to any matters which may be relevant to the functions of the Board;

d) The Commission shall, on any matter referred to it by the Board under article twenty-two, paragraph one b), take such action as it deems appropriate;

e) The Commission may, in conformity with the procedures laid down in article twelve, amends Table I and Table II;

f) The Commission may draw the attention of non-parties to decisions and recommendations which it adopts under this Convention, with a view to their considering taking action in accordance therewith.

Article Twenty-two

Functions of the Board

1. Without prejudice to the functions of the Commission under article twenty-one and without prejudice to the functions of the Board and the Commission under the 1961 Convention, the 1961 Convention as amended, and the 1971 Convention:

a) If, on the basis of its examination of information available to it, to the Secretary-General or to the Commission, or of information communicated by United Nations organs, the Board has reason to believe that the aims of this

Convention in matters related to its competence are not being met, the Board may invite a party or parties to furnish any relevant information;

b) With respect to articles twelve, thirteen, and sixteen:

i) After taking action under subparagraph a) of this article, the Board, if satisfied that it is necessary to do so, may call upon the party concerned to adopt such remedial measures as shall seem under the circumstances to be necessary for the execution of the provisions of articles twelve, thirteen, and sixteen;

ii) Prior to taking action under iii) below, the Board shall treat as confidential its communications with the party concerned under the preceding subparagraphs;

iii) If the Board finds that the party concerned has not taken remedial measures which it has been called upon to take under this subparagraph, it may call the attention of the parties, the Council, and the Commission to the matter. Any report published by the Board under this subparagraph shall also contain the views of the party concerned if the latter so requests.

2. Any party shall be invited to be represented at a meeting of the Board at which a question of direct interest to it is to be considered under this article.

3. If in any case, a decision of the Board which is adopted under this article is not unanimous, the views of the minority shall be stated.

4. Decisions of the Board under this article shall be taken by a two-thirds majority of the whole number of the Board.

5. In carrying out its functions pursuant to subparagraph one a) of this article, the Board shall ensure the confidentiality of all information which may come into its possession.

6. The Board's responsibility under this article shall not apply to the implementation of treaties or agreements entered into between parties in accordance with the provisions of this convention.

7. The provisions of this article shall not be applicable to disputes between parties falling under the provisions of article thirty-two.

Article Twenty-three

Reports of the Board

1. The Board shall prepare an annual report on its work, containing an analysis of the information at its disposal and in appropriate cases, an account of the explanations, if any, given by or required of parties, together with any observations and recommendations which the Board desires to make. The Board may make such additional reports as it considers necessary. The reports shall be submitted to the Council through the Commission which may make such comments as it sees fit.

2. The reports of the Board shall be communicated to the parties and subsequently published by the Secretary-General. The parties shall permit their unrestricted distribution.

Article Twenty-four

Application of stricter measures than those required by this convention

A party may adopt more strict or severe measures than those provided by this Convention if, in its opinion, such measures are desirable or necessary for the prevention or suppression of illicit traffic.

Article Twenty-five

Non-derogation from earlier treaty rights and obligations

The provisions of this Convention shall not derogate from any rights enjoyed or obligations undertaken by parties to this Convention under the 1961 Convention, the 1961 Convention as amended, and the 1971 Convention.

Article Twenty-six

Signature

This Convention shall be open for signature at the United Nations Office at Vienna from 20 December 1988 to 28 February 1989 and thereafter at the Headquarters of the United Nations at New York until 20 December 1989 by:

a) All states;
b) Namibia, represented by the United Nations Council for Namibia;
c) Regional economic integration organizations which have competence in respect of the negotiation, conclusion, application of international agreements in matters covered by this Convention, and references under the Convention to parties, states, or national services being applicable to these organizations within the limits of their competence.

Article Twenty-seven

Ratification, acceptance, approval, or act of formal confirmation

1. This Convention is subject to ratification, acceptance, or approval by states and by Namibia, represented by the United Nations Council for Namibia and to acts of formal confirmation by regional economic integration organizations referred to in article twenty-six, subparagraph c). The instruments of ratification, acceptance, approval, and those relating to acts of formal confirmation shall be deposited with the Secretary-General.

2. In their instruments of formal confirmation, regional economic integration organizations shall declare the extent of their competence with respect to the matters governed by this Convention. These organizations shall also inform the Secretary-General of any modification in the extent of their competence with respect to the matters governed by the Convention.

Article Twenty-eight

Accession

1. This Convention shall remain open for accession by any state, by Namibia, represented by the United Nations Council for Namibia, and by regional economic integration organizations referred to in article twenty-six, subparagraph c). Accession shall be effected by the deposit of an instrument of accession with the Secretary-General.

2. In their instruments of accession, regional economic integration organizations shall declare the extent of their competence with respect to the matters governed by this Convention. These organizations shall also inform the Secretary-General of any modification in the extent of

their competence with respect to the matters governed by the Convention.

Article Twenty-nine

Entry into force

1. This Convention shall enter into force on the ninetieth day after the date of the deposit with the Secretary-General of the twentieth instrument of ratification, acceptance, approval, or accession by states or by Namibia, represented by the Council for Namibia.

2. For each state or for Namibia, represented by the Council for Namibia, ratifying, accepting, approving, or acceding to this Convention after the deposit of the twentieth instrument of ratification, acceptance, approval, or accession, the Convention shall enter into force on the ninetieth day after the date of the deposit of its instrument of ratification, acceptance, approval, or accession.

3. For each regional economic integration organization referred to in article twenty-six, subparagraph c) depositing an instrument relating to an act of formal confirmation or an instrument of accession, this Convention shall enter into force on the ninetieth day after such deposit or at the date the Convention enters into force pursuant to paragraph one of this article, whichever is later.

Article Thirty

Denunciation

1. A party may denounce this Convention at any time by a written notification addressed to the Secretary-General.

2. Such denunciation shall take effect for the party concerned one year after the date of receipt of the notification by the Secretary-General.

Article Thirty-one

Amendments

1. Any party may propose an amendment to this Convention. The text of any such amendment and the reasons therefore shall be communicated by that party to the Secretary-General who shall communicate it to the other parties and shall ask them whether they accept the proposed amendment. If a proposed amendment so circulated has not been rejected by any party within twenty-four months after it has been circulated, it shall be deemed to have been accepted and shall enter into force in respect of a party, ninety days after that party has deposited with the Secretary-General an instrument expressing its consent to be bound by that amendment.

2. If a proposed amendment has been rejected by any party, the Secretary-General shall consult with the parties and if a majority so requests, he shall bring the matter, together with any comments made by the parties, before the Council which may decide to call a conference in accordance with article sixty-two, paragraph four of the Charter of the United Nations. Any amendment resulting from such a Conference shall be embodied in a Protocol of Amendment. Consent to be bound by such a protocol shall be required to be expressed specifically to the Secretary-General.

Article Thirty-two

Settlement of disputes

1. If there should arise between two or more parties a dispute relating to the interpretation or application of this Convention, the parties shall consult together with a view to the settlement of the dispute by negotiation, enquiry, mediation, conciliation, arbitration, recourse to regional bodies, judicial process, or other peaceful means of their own choice.
2. Any such dispute which cannot be settled in the manner prescribed in paragraph one of this article shall be referred, at the request of any one of the states parties to the dispute, to the International Court of Justice for decision.
3. If a regional economic integration organization referred to in article twenty-six, subparagraph c) is a party to a dispute which cannot be settled in the manner prescribed in paragraph one of this article, it may, through a State Member of the United Nations, request the Council to request an advisory opinion of the International Court of Justice in accordance with article sixty-five of the Statute of the Court, which opinion shall be regarded as decisive.
4. Each state, at the time of signature or ratification, acceptance, approval of this Convention, or accession thereto, or each regional economic integration organization, at the time of signature or deposit of an act of formal confirmation or accession, may declare that it does not consider itself bound by paragraphs two and three of this article. The other parties shall not be bound by paragraphs two and three with respect to any party having made such a declaration.
5. Any party having made a declaration in accordance with paragraph four of this article may at any time withdraw the declaration by notification to the Secretary-General.

Article Thirty-three

Authentic texts

The Arabic, Chinese, English, French, Russian, and Spanish texts of this convention are equally authentic.

Article Thirty-four

Depositary

The Secretary-General shall be the depositary of this Convention. In witness whereof, the undersigned, being duly authorized thereto, have signed this Convention. Done at Vienna, in one original, this twentieth day of December one thousand nine hundred and eighty-eight.

International Convention for the Suppression of the Financing of Terrorism Preamble, United Nations 1999

The states parties to this Convention,

Bearing in mind the purposes and principles of the Charter of the United Nations concerning the maintenance of international peace and security and the promotion of good neighborliness and friendly relations, and cooperation among states, deeply concerned about the worldwide escalation of acts of terrorism in all its forms and manifestations, Recalling the Declaration on the Occasion of the Fiftieth Anniversary of the United Nations, contained in General Assembly resolution 50/6 of 24 October 1995,

Recalling also all the relevant General Assembly resolutions on the matter, including resolution 49/60 of 9 December 1994 and its annex on the Declaration on Measures to Eliminate International Terrorism, in which the States Members of the United Nations solemnly reaffirmed their unequivocal condemnation of all acts, methods, and practices of terrorism as criminal and unjustifiable, wherever and by whomever committed, including those which jeopardize the friendly relations among states and peoples and threaten the territorial integrity and security of states,

Noting that the Declaration on Measures to Eliminate International Terrorism also encouraged states to review urgently the scope of the existing international legal provisions on the prevention, repression, and elimination of terrorism in all its forms and manifestations, with the aim of ensuring that there is a comprehensive legal framework covering all aspects of the matter, Recalling General Assembly resolution 51/210 of 17 December 1996, paragraph three, subparagraph (f), in which the assembly called upon all states to take steps to prevent and counteract, through appropriate domestic measures, the financing of terrorists and terrorist organizations, whether such financing is direct or indirect through organizations which also have or claim to have charitable, social, or cultural goals or which are also engaged

189

in unlawful activities such as illicit arms trafficking, drug dealing, and racketeering, including the exploitation of persons for purposes of funding terrorist activities, and in particular to consider, when appropriate, adopting regulatory measures to prevent and counteract movements of funds suspected to be intended for terrorist purposes without impeding in any way the freedom of legitimate capital movements and to intensify the exchange of information concerning international movements of such funds,

Recalling also General Assembly resolution 52/165 of 15 December 1997, in which the Assembly called upon states to consider, in particular, the implementation of the measures set out in paragraphs three (a) to (f) of its resolution 51/210 of 17 December 1996,

Recalling further General Assembly resolution 53/108 of 8 December 1998, in which the Assembly decided that the Ad Hoc Committee established by General Assembly resolution 51/210 of 17 December 1996 should elaborate a draft international convention for the suppression of terrorist financing to supplement related existing international instruments,

Considering that the financing of terrorism is a matter of grave concern to the international community as a whole, noting that the number and seriousness of acts of international terrorism depend on the financing that terrorists may obtain, noting also that existing multilateral legal instruments do not expressly address such financing,

Being convinced of the urgent need to enhance international cooperation among states in devising and adopting effective measures for the prevention of the financing of terrorism, as well as for its suppression through the prosecution and punishment of its perpetrators,

Have agreed as follows:

Article One

For the purposes of this Convention:
1. Funds mean assets of every kind, whether tangible or intangible, movable or immovable, however acquired, and legal documents or instruments in any form, including electronic or digital, evidencing title to, or interest in, such assets, including, but not limited to, bank credits, traveller's cheques, bank cheques, money orders, shares, securities, bonds, drafts, and letters of credit.

2. A state or governmental facility means any permanent or temporary facility or conveyance that is used or occupied by representatives of a state, members of government, the legislature, the judiciary, by officials or employees of a state, any other public authority or entity, or by employees or officials of an intergovernmental organization in connection with their official duties.

3. Proceeds mean any funds derived from or obtained, directly or indirectly, through the commission of an offence set forth in article two.

Article Two

1. Any person commits an offence within the meaning of this Convention, if that person by any means, directly or indirectly, unlawfully and willfully, provides or collects funds with the intention that they should be used or in the knowledge that they are to be used, in full or in part, in order to carry out:

(a) An act which constitutes an offence within the scope of and as defined in one of the treaties listed in the annex; or (b) Any other act intended to cause death or serious bodily injury to a civilian, or to any other person not taking an active part in the hostilities in a situation of armed conflict, when the purpose of such act, by its nature or context, is to intimidate a population, or to compel a government or an international organization to do or to abstain from doing any act.

2. (a) On depositing its instrument of ratification, acceptance, approval, or accession, a State Party which is not a party to a treaty listed in the annex may declare that, in the application of this Convention to the State Party, the treaty shall be deemed not to be included in the annex referred to in paragraph one, sub-paragraph (a). The declaration shall cease to have effect as soon as the treaty enters into force for the State Party, which shall notify the depositary of this fact;

(b) When a State Party ceases to be a party to a treaty listed in the annex, it may make a declaration as provided for in this article, with respect to that treaty

3. For an act to constitute an offence set forth in paragraph one, it shall not be necessary that the funds were actually used to carry out an offence referred to in paragraph one, subparagraphs (a) or (b);

4. Any person also commits an offence if that person attempts to commit an offence as set forth in paragraph one of this article;

5. Any person also commits an offence if that person:
(a) Participates as an accomplice in an offence as set forth in paragraph one or four of this article;

(b) Organizes or directs others to commit an offence as set forth in paragraph one or four of this article;

(c) Contributes to the commission of one or more offences as set forth in paragraphs one or four of this article by a group of persons acting with a common purpose. Such contribution shall be intentional and shall either:

Be made with the aim of furthering the criminal activity or criminal purpose of the group, where such activity or purpose involves the commission of an offence as set forth in paragraph one of this article or;

(ii) Be made in the knowledge of the intention of the group to commit an offence as set forth in paragraph one of this article.

Article Three

This Convention shall not apply where the offence is committed within a single state, the alleged offender is a national of that state and is present in the territory of that state, and no other state has a basis under article seven, paragraph one, or article seven, paragraph two, to exercise jurisdiction, except that the provisions of articles twelve to eighteen shall, as appropriate, apply in those cases.

Article Four

Each State Party shall adopt such measures as may be necessary:

(a) To establish as criminal offences under its domestic law the offences set forth in article two;

(b) To make those offences punishable by appropriate penalties which take into account the grave nature of the offences.

Article Five

1. Each state party, in accordance with its domestic legal principles, shall take the necessary measures to enable a legal entity located in its territory or organized under its laws to be held liable when a person responsible for the management or control of that legal entity has, in that capacity, committed an offence set forth in article two. Such liability may be criminal, civil, or administrative.

2. Such liability is incurred without prejudice to the criminal liability of individuals having committed the offences.

3. Each state party shall ensure, in particular, that legal entities liable in accordance with paragraph one above are subject to effective, proportionate, and dissuasive criminal, civil, or administrative sanctions. Such sanctions may include monetary sanctions.

Article Six

Each state party shall adopt such measures as may be necessary, including, when appropriate, domestic legislation, to ensure that criminal acts within the scope of this Convention are under no circumstances justifiable by considerations of a political, philosophical, ideological, racial, ethnical, religious, or other similar nature.

Article Seven

1. Each state party shall take such measures as may be necessary to establish its jurisdiction over the offences set forth in article two when:

(a) The offence is committed in the territory of that state;

(b) The offence is committed on board a vessel flying the flag of that state or an aircraft registered under the laws of that state at the time the offence is committed;

(c) The offence is committed by a national of that state.

2. A state party may also establish its jurisdiction over any such offence when:

(a) The offence was directed towards or resulted in the carrying out of an offence referred to in article two, paragraph one, subparagraph (a) or (b), in the territory of or against a national of that state;

(b) The offence was directed towards or resulted in the carrying out of an offence referred to in article two, paragraph one, subparagraph (a) or (b), against a state or government facility of that state abroad, including diplomatic or consular premises of that state;

(c) The offence was directed towards or resulted in an offence referred to in article two, paragraph one, subparagraph (a) or (b), committed in an attempt to compel that state to do or abstain from doing any act;

(d) The offence is committed by a stateless person who has his or her habitual residence in the territory of that state;

(e) The offence is committed on board an aircraft which is operated by the
government of that state.

3. Upon ratifying, accepting, approving, or acceding to this Convention, each state party shall notify the Secretary-General of the United Nations of the jurisdiction it has established in accordance with paragraph two. Should any change take place, the State Party concerned shall immediately notify the Secretary-General.

4. Each state party shall likewise take such measures as may be necessary to establish its jurisdiction over the offences set forth in article two in cases where the alleged offender is present in its territory, and it does not extradite that person to any of the States Parties that have established their jurisdiction in accordance with paragraphs one or two.

5. When more than one State Party claims jurisdiction over the offences set forth in article two, the relevant States Parties shall strive to coordinate their actions appropriately, in particular, concerning the conditions for prosecution and the modalities for mutual legal assistance.

6. Without prejudice to the norms of general international law, this Convention does not exclude the exercise of any criminal ju-

risdiction established by a State Party in accordance with its domestic law.

Article Eight

1. Each state party shall take appropriate measures, in accordance with its domestic legal principles, for the identification, detection, and freezing or seizure of any funds used or allocated for the purpose of committing the offences set forth in article two, as well as the proceeds derived from such offences, for purposes of possible forfeiture.

2. Each state party shall take appropriate measures, in accordance with its domestic legal principles, for the forfeiture of funds used or allocated for the purpose of committing the offences set forth in article two and the proceeds derived from such offences.

3. Each state party concerned may give consideration to concluding agreements on the sharing with other states parties, on a regular or case-by-case basis, of the funds derived from the forfeitures referred to in this article.

4. Each state party shall consider establishing mechanisms whereby the funds derived from the forfeitures referred to in this article are utilized to compensate the victims of offences referred to in article two, paragraph one, subparagraph (a) or (b), or their families.

5. The provisions of this article shall be implemented without prejudice to the rights of third parties acting in good faith.

Article Nine

1. Upon receiving information that a person who has committed or who is alleged to have committed an offence set forth in article two may be present in its territory, the State Party concerned shall take such measures as may be necessary under its domestic law to investigate the facts contained in the information.

2. Upon being satisfied that the circumstances so warrant, the state party in whose territory the offender or alleged offender is present shall take the appropriate measures under its domestic law so as to ensure that person's presence for the purpose of prosecution or extradition.

Any person regarding whom the measures referred to in paragraph two are being taken shall be entitled to:

(a) Communicate without delay with the nearest appropriate representative of the state of which that person is a national or which is otherwise entitled to protect that person's rights or, if that person is a stateless person, the state in the territory of which that person habitually resides;

(b) Be visited by a representative of that state;

(c) Be informed of that person's rights under subparagraphs (a) and (b).

4. The rights referred to in paragraph three shall be exercised in conformity with the laws and regulations of the state in the territory of which the offender or alleged offender is present, subject to the provision that the said laws and regulations must enable full effect to be given to the purposes for which the rights accorded under paragraph three are intended.

5. The provisions of paragraphs three and four shall be without prejudice to the right of any state party having a claim to jurisdiction in accordance with article seven, paragraph one, subparagraph (b) or paragraph two, subparagraph (b) to invite the International Committee of the Red Cross to communicate with and visit the alleged offender.

6. When a state party, pursuant to the present article, has taken a person into custody, it shall immediately notify, directly or through the Secretary-General of the United Nations, the states parties which have established jurisdiction in accordance with ar-

ticle seven, paragraph one or two and if it considers it advisable, any other interested states parties, of the fact that such person is in custody and of the circumstances which warrant that person's detention. The state which makes the investigation contemplated in paragraph one shall promptly inform the said States Parties of its findings and shall indicate whether it intends to exercise jurisdiction.

Article Ten

1. The state party in the territory of which the alleged offender is present shall, in cases to which article seven applies, if it does not extradite that person, be obliged, without exception, whatsoever and whether the offence was committed in its territory, to submit the case without undue delay to its competent authorities for the purpose of prosecution, through proceedings in accordance with the laws of that state. Those authorities shall take their decision in the same manner as in the case of any other offence of a grave nature under the law of that state.

2. Whenever a state party is permitted under its domestic law to extradite or otherwise surrender one of its nationals only upon the condition that the person will be returned to that state to serve the sentence imposed as a result of the trial or proceeding for which the extradition or surrender of the person was sought and this state and the state seeking the extradition of the person agree with this option and other terms they may deem appropriate, such a conditional extradition or surrender shall be sufficient to discharge the obligation set forth in paragraph one.

Article Eleven

1. The offences set forth in article two shall be deemed to be included as extraditable offences in any extradition treaty existing between any of the states parties before the entry into force of this convention. states parties undertake to include such offences as extraditable offences in every extradition treaty to be subsequently concluded between them.

2. When a state party which makes extradition conditional on the existence of a treaty receives a request for extradition from another state party with which it has no extradition treaty, the requested state party may, at its option, consider this convention as a legal basis for extradition in respect of the offences set forth in article two. Extradition shall be subject to the other conditions provided by the law of the requested state.

3. States parties which do not make extradition conditional on the existence of a treaty shall recognize the offences set forth in article two as extraditable offences between themselves, subject to the conditions provided by the law of the requested state.

4. If necessary, the offences set forth in article two shall be treated, for the purposes of extradition between States Parties, as if they had been committed not only in the place in which they occurred but also in the territory of the states that have established jurisdiction in accordance with article seven, paragraphs one and two.

5. The provisions of all extradition treaties and arrangements between states parties with regard to offences set forth in article two shall be deemed to be modified as between States Parties to the extent that they are incompatible with this convention.

Article Twelve
1. States parties shall afford one another the greatest measure of assistance in connection with criminal investigations or criminal or extradition proceedings in respect of the offences set forth in article two, including assistance in obtaining evidence in their possession necessary for the proceedings.

2. States parties may not refuse a request for mutual legal assistance on the ground of bank secrecy.

3. The requesting party shall neither transmit nor use information or evidence furnished by the requested party for investigations, prosecutions, or proceedings other than those stated in the request without the prior consent of the requested party.

Each state party may give consideration to establishing mechanisms to share with other states parties information or evidence needed to establish criminal, civil, or administrative liability pursuant to article five.

5. States parties shall carry out their obligations under paragraphs one and two in conformity with any treaties or other arrangements on mutual legal assistance or information exchange that may exist between them. In the absence of such treaties or arrangements, states parties shall afford one another assistance in accordance with their domestic law.

Article Thirteen

None of the offences set forth in article two shall be regarded, for the purposes of extradition or mutual legal assistance, as a fiscal offence. Accordingly, states parties may not refuse a request for extradition or for mutual legal assistance on the sole ground that it concerns a fiscal offence.

Article Fourteen

None of the offences set forth in article two shall be regarded for the purposes of extradition or mutual legal assistance as a political offence or as an offence connected with a political offence or as an offence inspired by political motives. Accordingly, a request for extradition or for mutual legal assistance based on such an offence may not be refused on the sole ground that it concerns a political offence or an offence connected with a political offence or an offence inspired by political motives.

Article Fifteen

Nothing in this Convention shall be interpreted as imposing an obligation to extradite or to afford mutual legal assistance if the requested State Party has substantial grounds for believing that the request for extradition for offences set forth in article two or for mutual legal assistance with respect to such offences has been made for the purpose of prosecuting or punishing a person on account of that person's race, religion, nationality, ethnic origin, or political opinion or that compliance with the request would cause prejudice to that person's position for any of these reasons.

Article Sixteen

1. A person who is being detained or is serving a sentence in the territory of one State Party whose presence in another State Party is requested for purposes of identification, testimony, or otherwise providing assistance in obtaining evidence for the investigation or prosecution of offences set forth in article two may be transferred if the following conditions are met:

The person freely gives his or her informed consent;

(a) The competent authorities of both states agree, subject to such conditions as those states may deem appropriate.

2. For the purposes of the present article:

(a) The state to which the person is transferred shall have the authority and obligation to keep the person transferred in custody, unless otherwise requested or authorized by the state from which the person was transferred;

(b) The state to which the person is transferred shall, without delay, implement its obligation to return the person to the custody of the state from which the person was transferred as agreed beforehand, or as otherwise agreed, by the competent authorities of both states;

(c) The state to which the person is transferred shall not require the state from which the person was transferred to initiate extradition proceedings for the return of the person;

(d) The person transferred shall receive credit for service of the sentence being served in the state from which he or she was transferred for time spent in the custody of the state to which he or she was transferred.

3. Unless the State Party from which a person is to be transferred in accordance with the present article so agrees, that person, whatever his or her nationality, shall not be prosecuted or detained or subjected to any other restriction of his or her personal liberty in the territory of the state to which that person is transferred in respect of acts or convictions anterior to his or her departure from the territory of the state from which such person was transferred.

Article Seventeen

Any person who is taken into custody or regarding whom any other measures are taken or proceedings are carried out pursuant to this Convention shall be guaranteed fair treatment, including enjoyment of all rights and guarantees in conformity with the law of the state in the territory of which that person is present and applicable provisions of international law, including international human rights law.

Article Eighteen

1. States Parties shall cooperate in the prevention of the offences set forth in article two by taking all practicable measures, *inter alia*, by adapting their domestic legislation, if necessary, to prevent and counter preparations in their respective territories for the commission of those offences within or outside their territories including:

(a) Measures to prohibit in their territories illegal activities of persons and organizations that knowingly encourage, instigate, organize, or engage in the commission of offences set forth in article two;
(b) Measures requiring financial institutions and other professions involved in financial transactions to utilize the most efficient measures available for the identification of their usual or

occasional customers, as well as customers in whose interest accounts are opened, to pay special attention to unusual or suspicious transactions, and report transactions suspected of stemming from a criminal activity.
For this purpose, States Parties shall consider:

(i) Adopting regulations prohibiting the opening of accounts the holders or beneficiaries of which are unidentified or unidentifiable and measures to ensure that such institutions verify the identity of the real owners of such transactions;

(ii) With respect to the identification of legal entities, requiring financial institutions,
when necessary, to take measures to verify the legal existence and the structure of the customer by obtaining, either from a public register or from the customer or both, proof of incorporation, including information concerning the customer's name, legal form, address, directors, and provisions regulating the power to bind the entity;

(iii) Adopting regulations imposing on financial institutions the obligation to report promptly to the competent authorities all complex, unusual large transactions, and unusual patterns of transactions, which have no apparent economic or obviously lawful purpose, without fear of assuming criminal or civil liability for breach of any restriction on disclosure of information if they report their suspicions in good faith and;

(iv) Requiring financial institutions to maintain, for at least five years, all necessary records on transactions, both domestic or international.

2. States parties shall further cooperate in the prevention of offences set forth in article two by considering:

(a) Measures for the supervision, including, for example, the licensing of all money transmission agencies;

(b) Feasible measures to detect or monitor the physical cross-border transportation of cash and bearer negotiable instruments, subject to strict safeguards to ensure proper use of information, and without impeding in any way the freedom of capital movements.

3. States parties shall further cooperate in the prevention of the offences set forth in article two by exchanging accurate and verified information in accordance with their domestic law and co-ordinating administrative and other measures taken, as appropriate, to prevent the commission of offences set forth in article two in particular by:

(a) Establishing and maintaining channels of communication between their competent agencies and services to facilitate the secure and rapid exchange of information concerning all aspects of offences set forth in article two;

(b) Cooperating with one another in conducting inquiries, with respect to the offences set forth in article two concerning:

(i) The identity, whereabouts, and activities of persons in respect of whom reasonable suspicion exists that they are involved in such offences and;
(ii) The movement of funds relating to the commission of such offences.

4. States Parties may exchange information through the International Criminal Police Organization (Interpol).

Article Nineteen

The state party where the alleged offender is prosecuted shall, in accordance with its domestic law or applicable procedures, communicate the final outcome of the proceedings to the Secretary-General of the United Nations, who shall transmit the information to the other states parties.

Article Twenty

The states parties shall carry out their obligations under this Convention in a manner consistent with the principles of sovereign equality and territorial integrity of states and that of non-intervention in the domestic affairs of other states.

Article Twenty-one

Nothing in this Convention shall affect other rights, obligations, and responsibilities of states and individuals under international law, in particular the purposes of the Charter of the United Nations, international humanitarian law, and other relevant conventions.

Article Twenty-two

Nothing in this Convention entitles a state party to undertake in the territory of another State Party the exercise of jurisdiction or performance of functions which are exclusively reserved for the authorities of that other State Party by its domestic law.

Article Twenty-three

1. The annex may be amended by the addition of relevant treaties that:
(a) Are open to the participation of all states;
(b) Have entered into force and;
(c) Have been ratified, accepted, approved, or acceded to by at least twenty-two States Parties to the present Convention.

2. After the entry into force of this Convention, any state party may propose such an amendment. Any proposal for an amendment shall be communicated to the depositary in written form. The depositary shall notify proposals that meet the requirements of paragraph one to all states parties and seek their views on whether the proposed amendment should be adopted.

3. The proposed amendment shall be deemed adopted unless one third of the states parties object to it by a written notification not later than 180 days after its circulation.

4. The adopted amendment to the annex shall enter into force thirty days after the deposit of the twenty-second instrument of ratification, acceptance, or approval of such amendment for all those states parties having deposited such an instrument. For each state party ratifying, accepting, or approving the amendment after the deposit of the twenty-second instrument, the amendment shall enter into force on the thirtieth day after deposit by such state party of its instrument of ratification, acceptance, or approval.

Article Twenty-four

1. Any dispute between two or more States Parties concerning the interpretation or application of this Convention which cannot be settled through negotiation within a reasonable time shall, at the request of one of them, be submitted to arbitration. If, within six months from the date of the request for arbitration, the parties are unable to agree on the organization of the arbitration, any one of those parties may refer the dispute to the International Court of Justice, by application, in conformity with the Statute of the Court.

2. Each state may at the time of signature, ratification, acceptance, or approval of this Convention or accession thereto declare that it does not consider itself bound by paragraph one. The other states parties shall not be bound by paragraph one with respect to any state party which has made such a reservation.

3. Any state which has made a reservation in accordance with paragraph two may, at any time, withdraw that reservation by notification to the Secretary-General of the United Nations.

Article Twenty-five

1. This Convention shall be open for signature by all states from 10 January 2000 to 31 December 2001 at United Nations Headquarters in New York.

2. This Convention is subject to ratification, acceptance, or approval. The instruments of ratification, acceptance, or approval shall be deposited to the Secretary-General of the United Nations.

3. This Convention shall be open to accession by any state. The instruments of accession shall be deposited to the Secretary-General of the United Nations.

Article Twenty-six

1. This Convention shall enter into force on the thirtieth day following the date of the deposit of the twenty-second instrument of ratification, acceptance, approval, or accession to the Secretary-General of the United Nations.

2. For each state ratifying, accepting, approving, or acceding to the Convention after the deposit of the twenty-second instrument of ratification, acceptance, approval, or accession, the Convention shall enter into force on the thirtieth day after deposit by such state of its instrument of ratification, acceptance, approval, or accession.

Article Twenty-seven

1. Any state party may denounce this Convention by written notification to the Secretary-General of the United Nations.

2. Denunciation shall take effect one year following the date on which notification is received by the Secretary-General of the United Nations.

Article Twenty-eight

The original of this convention, of which the Arabic, Chinese, English, French, Russian, and Spanish texts are equally authentic, shall be deposited to the Secretary-General of the United Nations who shall send certified copies thereof to all states.

In witness whereof, the undersigned, being duly authorized thereto by their respective governments, have signed this Convention, opened for signature at United Nations Headquarters in New York on 10 January 2000.

Annex

1. Convention for the Suppression of Unlawful Seizure of Aircraft, done at The Hague on 16 December 1970.
2. Convention for the Suppression of Unlawful Acts against the Safety of Civil Aviation, done at Montreal on 23 September 1971.
3. Convention on the Prevention and Punishment of Crimes against Internationally Protected Persons, including Diplomatic Agents, adopted by the General Assembly of the United Nations on 14 December 1973.
4. International Convention against the Taking of Hostages, adopted by the General Assembly of the United Nations on 17 December 1979.
5. Convention on the Physical Protection of Nuclear Material, adopted at Vienna on 3 March 1980.
6. Protocol for the Suppression of Unlawful Acts of Violence at Airports Serving International Civil Aviation, supplementary to the Convention for the Suppression of Unlawful Acts against the Safety of Civil Aviation, done at Montreal on 24 February 1988.
7. Convention for the Suppression of Unlawful Acts against the Safety of Maritime Navigation, done at Rome on 10 March 1988.
8. Protocol for the Suppression of Unlawful Acts against the Safety of Fixed Platforms located on the Continental Shelf, done at Rome on 10 March 1988.
9. International Convention for the Suppression of Terrorist Bombings, adopted by the General Assembly of the United Nations on 15 December 1997.

Appendix III - 40+9 Special Recommendation to combat terrorist financing

The Forty Recommendations provide a complete set of counter-measures against money laundering, covering the criminal justice system and law enforcement, the financial system and its regulation, and international co-operation. They have been recognized, endorsed, or adopted by many international bodies. The recommendations are neither complex nor difficult, nor do they compromise the freedom to engage in legitimate transactions or threaten economic development. They set out the principles for action and allow countries a measure of flexibility in implementing these principles according to their particular circumstances and constitutional frameworks. Though not a binding international convention, many countries in the world have made a political commitment to combat money laundering by implementing the Forty Recommendations.

Initially developed in 1990, the recommendations were revised for the first time in 1996 to take into account changes in money laundering trends and to anticipate potential future threats. More recently, the FATF has completed a thorough review and update of the Forty Recommendations (2003). The FATF has also elaborated various Interpretative Notes which are designed to clarify the application of specific recommendations and to provide additional guidance. Below are the Forty and Nine Recommendations and their Interpretive Notes:

The Forty Recommendations

Introduction

Money laundering methods and techniques change in response to developing counter-measures. In recent years, the Financial Action Task Force (FATF) has noted increasingly sophisticated combinations of techniques, such as the increased use of legal persons to disguise the true ownership and control of illegal proceeds and an increased use of professionals to provide advice and assistance in laundering criminal funds. These factors, combined with the experience gained through the FATF's Non-Cooperative Countries and Territories process and a number of national and international initiatives, led the FATF to review and revise the Forty Recommendations into a new comprehensive framework for combating money laundering and terrorist financing. The FATF now calls upon all countries to take the necessary steps to bring their national systems for combating money laundering and terrorist financing into compliance with the new FATF Recommendations and to effectively implement these measures.

The review process for revising the Forty Recommendations was an extensive one open to FATF members, non-members, observers, financial, and other affected sectors and interested parties. This consultation process provided a wide range of input, all of which was considered in the review process.

The revised Forty Recommendations now apply not only to money laundering but also to terrorist financing, and when combined with the Nine Special Recommendations on Terrorist Financing provide an enhanced, comprehensive, and consistent framework of measures for combating money laundering and terrorist financing. The FATF recognizes that countries have diverse legal and financial systems and so all cannot take identical measures to achieve the common objective, especially over matters of detail. The Recommendations therefore set minimum standards for action for countries to implement the detail according to their particular circumstances and constitutional frameworks. The recommendations cover all the measures that national systems should have in place within their criminal justice and regulatory systems, the preventive measures to be taken by financial institutions and certain other businesses, professions, and international co-operation.

The original FATF Forty Recommendations were drawn up in 1990 as an initiative to combat the misuse of financial systems by persons laundering drug money. In 1996, the recommendations were revised for the first time to reflect evolving money laundering typologies. The 1996, Forty Recommendations have been endorsed by more than 130 countries and the international anti-money laundering standard.

In October 2001, the FATF expanded its mandate to deal with the issue of the financing of terrorism and took the important step of creating the Nine Special Recommendations on Terrorist Financing. These recommendations contain a set of measures aimed at combating the funding of terrorist acts and terrorist organizations and are complementary to the Forty Recommendations.

A key element in the fight against money laundering and the financing of terrorism is the need for countries systems to be monitored and evaluated with respect to these international standards. The mutual evaluations conducted by the FATF and FATF-style regional bodies, as well as the assessments conducted by the IMF and World Bank are a vital mechanism for ensuring that the FATF Recommendations are effectively implemented by all countries.

Legal Systems: Scope of the criminal offence of money laundering

Recommendation One
Countries should criminalize money laundering on the basis of United Nations Convention against Illicit Traffic in Narcotic

Drugs and Psychotropic Substances 1988 (the Vienna Convention) and United Nations Convention against Transnational Organized Crime 2000 (the Palermo Convention).

Countries should apply the crime of money laundering to all serious offences, with a view to including the widest range of predicate offences. Predicate offences may be described by reference to all offences, or to a threshold linked either to a category of serious offences or to the penalty of imprisonment applicable to the predicate offence (threshold approach), or to a list of predicate offences, or a combination of these approaches.

Where countries apply a threshold approach, predicate offences should, at a minimum, comprise all offences that fall within the category of serious offences under their national law or should include offences which are punishable by a maximum penalty of more than one year imprisonment or for those countries that have a minimum threshold for offences in their legal system, predicate offences should comprise all offences, which are punished by a minimum penalty of more than six months imprisonment.

Whichever approach is adopted, each country should, at a minimum, include a range of offences within each of the designated categories of offences [3].

Predicate offences for money laundering should extend to conduct that occurred in another country, which constitutes an offence in that country, and which would have constituted a predicate offence had it occurred domestically. Countries may provide that the only prerequisite is that the conduct would have constituted a predicate offence had it occurred domestically. Countries may provide that the offence of money laundering does not apply to persons who committed the predicate offence, where this is required by fundamental principles of their domestic law.

Recommendation Two
Countries should ensure that:

a) The intent and knowledge required to prove the offence of money laundering is consistent with the standards set forth in the Vienna and Palermo Conventions, including the concept that such mental state may be inferred from objective factual circumstances.

b) Criminal liability, and, where that is not possible, civil or administrative liability, should apply to legal persons. This should not preclude parallel criminal, civil, or administrative proceedings with respect to legal persons in countries in which such forms of liability are available. Legal persons should be subject to effective, proportionate, and dissuasive sanctions. Such measures should be without prejudice to the criminal liability of individuals.

Provisional measures and confiscation
Recommendation Three
Countries should adopt measures similar to those set forth in the Vienna and Palermo Conventions, including legislative measures, to enable their competent authorities to confiscate property laundered, proceeds from money laundering or predicate offences, instrumentalities used in or intended for use in the commission of these offences, or property of corresponding value without prejudicing the rights of bona fide third parties.

Such measures should include the authority to: (a) identify, trace, and evaluate property which is subject to confiscation; (b) carry out provisional measures, such as freezing and seizing, to prevent any dealing, transfer, or disposal of such property; (c) take steps that will prevent or void actions that prejudice the state's ability to recover property that is subject to confiscation; and (d) take any appropriate investigative measures.

Countries may consider adopting measures that allow such proceeds or instrumentalities to be confiscated without requiring a criminal conviction or which require an offender to demonstrate

the lawful origin of the property alleged to be liable to confiscation to the extent that such a requirement is consistent with the principles of their domestic law.
Measures to be taken by Financial Institutions and Non-Financial Businesses and Professions to prevent Money Laundering and Terrorist Financing

Customer due diligence and record keeping
Recommendation Four
Countries should ensure that financial institution secrecy laws do not inhibit implementation of the FATF Recommendations.

Recommendation Five
Financial institutions should not keep anonymous accounts or accounts in obviously fictitious names. Financial institutions should undertake customer due diligence measures, including identifying and verifying the identity of their customers, when establishing business relations and carrying out occasional transactions: (i) above the applicable designated threshold or; (ii) that are wire transfers in the circumstances covered by the Interpretative Note to Special Recommendation VII; there is a suspicion of money laundering or terrorist financing or the financial institution has doubts about the veracity or adequacy of previously obtained customer identification data.

The customer due diligence (CDD) measures to be taken are as follows:

a) Identifying the customer and verifying the customer's identity using reliable, independent source documents, data, or information [4].

b) Identifying the beneficial owner and taking reasonable measures to verify the identity of the beneficial owner such that the financial institution is satisfied that it knows who the beneficial owner is. For legal persons and arrangements, this should include financial institutions taking reasonable measures to understand the ownership and control structure of the customer.

c) Obtaining information on the purpose and intended nature of the business relationship.

d) Conducting ongoing due diligence on the business relationship and scrutiny of transactions undertaken throughout the course of that relationship to ensure that the transactions being conducted are consistent with the institution's knowledge of the customer, their business, and risk profile, including, where necessary, the source of funds.

Financial institutions should apply each of the CDD measures under (a) to (d) above but may determine the extent of such measures on a risk sensitive basis depending on the type of customer, business relationship, or transaction. The measures that are taken should be consistent with any guidelines issued by competent authorities. For higher risk categories, financial institutions should perform enhanced due diligence. In certain circumstances, where there are low risks, countries may decide that financial institutions can apply reduced or simplified measures.

Financial institutions should verify the identity of the customer and beneficial owner before or during the course of establishing a business relationship or conducting transactions for occasional customers. Countries may permit financial institutions to complete the verification as soon as reasonably practicable following the establishment of the relationship, where the money laundering risks are effectively managed and where this is essential not to interrupt the normal conduct of business.

Where the financial institution is unable to comply with paragraphs (a) to (c) above, it should not open the account, commence business relations, or perform the transaction, or it should terminate the business relationship, and should consider making a suspicious transactions report in relation to the customer.

These requirements should apply to all new customers, though financial institutions should also apply this recommendation to existing customers on the basis of materiality and risk, and should conduct due diligence on such existing relationships at appropriate times.

Recommendation Six

Financial institutions should, in relation to Politically Exposed Persons, in addition to performing normal due diligence measures:

a) Have appropriate risk management systems to determine whether the customer is a Politically Exposed Person.
b) Obtain senior management approval for establishing business relationships with such customers.
c) Take reasonable measures to establish the source of wealth and source of funds.
d) Conduct enhanced ongoing monitoring of the business relationship.

Recommendation Seven

Financial institutions should, in relation to cross-border correspondent banking and other similar relationships, in addition to performing normal due diligence measures:

a) Gather sufficient information about a respondent institution to understand fully the nature of the respondent's business and to determine from publicly available information the reputation of the institution and the quality of supervision, including whether it has been subject to a money laundering or terrorist financing investigation or regulatory action.
b) Assess the respondent institution's anti-money laundering and terrorist financing controls.
c) Obtain approval from senior management before establishing new correspondent relationships.
d) Document the respective responsibilities of each institution.

e) With respect to "payable-through accounts," be satisfied that the respondent bank has verified the identity of and performed on-going due diligence on the customers having direct access to accounts of the correspondent and that it is able to provide relevant customer identification data upon request to the correspondent bank.

Recommendation Eight

Financial institutions should pay special attention to any money laundering threats that may arise from new or developing technologies that might favour anonymity and take measures, if needed, to prevent their use in money laundering schemes. In particular, financial institutions should have policies and procedures in place to address any specific risks associated with non-face to face business relationships or transactions.

Recommendation Nine

Countries may permit financial institutions to rely on intermediaries or other third parties to perform elements (a) and (c) of the CDD process or to introduce business, provided that the criteria set out below are met. Where such reliance is permitted, the ultimate responsibility for customer identification and verification remains with the financial institution relying on the third party. The criteria that should be met are as follows:

a) A financial institution relying upon a third party should immediately obtain the necessary information concerning elements (a) and (c) of the CDD process. Financial institutions should take adequate steps to satisfy themselves that copies of identification data and other relevant documentation relating to the CDD requirements will be made available from the third party upon request without delay.

b) The financial institution should satisfy itself that the third party is regulated and supervised for and has measures in place to comply with CDD requirements in line with Recommendations five and ten.

It is left to each country to determine in which countries the third party that meets the conditions can be based, having regard to information available on countries that do not or do not adequately apply the FATF Recommendations.

Recommendation Ten

Financial institutions should maintain, for at least five years, all necessary records on transactions, both domestic or international, to enable them to comply swiftly with information requests from the competent authorities. Such records must be sufficient to permit reconstruction of individual transactions (including the amounts and types of currency involved if any) so as to provide, if necessary, evidence for prosecution of criminal activity.

Financial institutions should keep records on the identification data obtained through the customer due diligence process (e.g. copies or records of official identification documents like passports, identity cards, driving licenses, or similar documents), account files and business correspondence for at least five years after the business relationship is ended.

The identification data and transaction records should be available to domestic competent authorities upon appropriate authority.

Recommendation Eleven

Financial institutions should pay special attention to all complex, unusual large transactions, and all unusual patterns of transactions, which have no apparent economic or visible lawful purpose. The background and purpose of such transactions should, as far as possible, be examined, the findings established in writing and be available to help competent authorities and auditors.

Recommendation Twelve

The customer due diligence and record-keeping requirements set out in Recommendations five, six, and eight to eleven apply to designated non-financial businesses and professions in the following situations:

a) Casinos: when customers engage in financial transactions equal to or above the applicable designated threshold.
b) Real estate agents: when they are involved in transactions for their client concerning the buying and selling of real estate.
c) Dealers in precious metals and dealers in precious stones: when they engage in any cash transaction with a customer equal to or above the applicable designated threshold.
d) Lawyers, notaries, other independent legal professionals, and accountants: when they prepare for or carry out transactions for their client concerning the following activities:
   - buying and selling of real estate;
   - managing of client money, securities, or other assets;
   - management of bank, savings, or securities accounts;
   - organization of contributions for the creation, operation, or management of companies;
   - creation, operation or management of legal persons or arrangements, and buying and selling of business entities.
e) Trust and company service providers: when they prepare for or carry out transactions for a client concerning the activities listed in the definition in the Glossary.

Reporting of suspicious transactions and compliance

Recommendation Thirteen
If a financial institution suspects or has reasonable grounds to suspect that funds are the proceeds of a criminal activity or are related to terrorist financing, it should be required, directly by law or regulation, to report promptly its suspicions to the financial intelligence unit (FIU).

Recommendation Fourteen
Financial institutions, their directors, officers, and employees should be:

a) Protected by legal provisions from criminal and civil liability for breach of any restriction on disclosure of information imposed by contract or by any legislative, regulatory or administrative provision, if they report their suspicions in good faith

to the FIU, even if they did not know precisely what the underlying criminal activity was, and regardless of whether illegal activity actually occurred.
b) Prohibited by law from disclosing the fact that a suspicious transaction report (STR) or related information is being reported to the FIU.

Recommendation Fifteen

Financial institutions should develop programs against money laundering and terrorist financing. These programs should include:

a) The development of internal policies, procedures and controls, including appropriate compliance management arrangements, and adequate screening procedures to ensure high standards when hiring employees.
b) An ongoing employee training program.
c) An audit function to test the system.

Recommendation Sixteen

The requirements set out in Recommendations thirteen to fifteen and twenty-one apply to all designated non-financial businesses and professions, subject to the following qualifications:

a) Lawyers, notaries, other independent legal professionals, and accountants should be required to report suspicious transactions when, on behalf of or for a client, they engage in a financial transaction in relation to the activities described in Recommendation twelve(d). Countries are strongly encouraged to extend the reporting requirement to the rest of the professional activities of accountants, including auditing.
b) Dealers in precious metals and dealers in precious stones should be required to report suspicious transactions when they engage in any cash transaction with a customer equal to or above the applicable designated threshold.
c) Trust and company service providers should be required to report suspicious transactions for a client when, on behalf of

or for a client, they engage in a transaction in relation to the activities referred to Recommendation twelve(e).

Lawyers, notaries, other independent legal professionals, and accountants acting as independent legal professionals, are not required to report their suspicions if the relevant information was obtained in circumstances where they are subject to professional secrecy or legal professional privilege.

Other measures to deter money laundering and terrorist financing

Recommendation Seventeen
Countries should ensure that effective, proportionate, and dissuasive sanctions, whether criminal, civil, or administrative, are available to deal with natural or legal persons covered by these Recommendations that fail to comply with anti-money laundering or terrorist financing requirements.

Recommendation Eighteen
Countries should not approve the establishment or accept the continued operation of shell banks. Financial institutions should refuse to enter into, or continue, a correspondent banking relationship with shell banks. Financial institutions should also guard against establishing relations with respondent foreign financial institutions that permit their accounts to be used by shell banks.

Recommendation Nineteen (This Recommendation was revised and the following text was issued on 22 October 2004)

Countries should consider the feasibility and utility of a system where banks and other financial institutions and intermediaries would report all domestic and international currency transactions above a fixed amount to a national central agency with a computerized data base, available to competent authorities for use in money laundering or terrorist financing cases, subject to strict safeguards to ensure proper use of the information.

Recommendation Twenty

Countries should consider applying the FATF Recommendations to businesses and professions other than designated non-financial businesses and professions that pose a money laundering or terrorist financing risk.

Countries should further encourage the development of modern and secure techniques of money management that are less vulnerable to money laundering.

Measures to be taken with respect to countries that do not or insufficiently comply with the FATF Recommendations

Recommendation Twenty-one

Financial institutions should give special attention to business relationships and transactions with persons, including companies and financial institutions, from countries which do not or insufficiently apply the FATF Recommendations. Whenever these transactions have no apparent economic or visible lawful purpose, their background and purpose should, as far as possible, be examined, the findings established in writing, and be made available to help competent authorities. Where such a country continues not to apply or insufficiently applies the FATF Recommendations, countries should be able to apply appropriate countermeasures.

Recommendation Twenty-two

Financial institutions should ensure that the principles applicable to financial institutions, which are mentioned above are also applied to branches and majority owned subsidiaries located abroad, especially in countries which do not or insufficiently apply the FATF Recommendations, to the extent that local applicable laws and regulations permit. When local applicable laws and regulations prohibit this implementation, competent authorities in the country of the parent institution should be informed by the financial institutions that they cannot apply the FATF Recommendations.

Regulation and supervision

Recommendation Twenty-three

Countries should ensure that financial institutions are subject to adequate regulation and supervision and are effectively implementing the FATF Recommendations. Competent authorities should take the necessary legal or regulatory measures to prevent criminals or their associates from holding or being the beneficial owner of a significant or controlling interest or holding a management function in a financial institution.

For financial institutions subject to the core principles, the regulatory and supervisory measures that apply for prudential purposes and which are also relevant to money laundering, should apply in a similar manner for anti-money laundering and terrorist financing purposes.

Other financial institutions should be licensed or registered, and appropriately regulated and subject to supervision or oversight for anti-money laundering purposes, having regard to the risk of money laundering or terrorist financing in that sector. At a minimum, businesses providing a service of money or value transfer or of money or currency changing, should be licensed or registered and subject to effective systems for monitoring and ensuring compliance with national requirements to combat money laundering and terrorist financing.

Recommendation Twenty-four

Designated non-financial businesses and professions should be subject to regulatory and supervisory measures as set out below.

a) Casinos should be subject to a comprehensive regulatory and supervisory regime that ensures that they have effectively implemented the necessary anti-money laundering and terrorist financing measures. At a minimum, casinos should be licensed;

competent authorities should take the necessary legal or regulatory measures to prevent criminals or their associates from holding or being the beneficial owner of a significant or controlling interest, holding a management function in, or being an operator of a casino; competent authorities should ensure that casinos are effectively supervised for compliance with requirements to combat money laundering and terrorist financing.

b) Countries should ensure that the other categories of designated non-financial businesses and professions are subject to effective systems for monitoring and ensuring their compliance with requirements to combat money laundering and terrorist financing. This should be performed on a risk-sensitivity basis. This may be performed by a government authority or by an appropriate self-regulatory organization, provided that such an organization can ensure that its members comply with their obligations to combat money laundering and terrorist financing.

Recommendation Twenty-five

The competent authorities should establish guidelines and provide feedback which will assist financial institutions and designated non-financial businesses and professions in applying national measures to combat money laundering and terrorist financing, and in particular, in detecting and reporting suspicious transactions. Institutional and other measures necessary in systems for combating money laundering and terrorist financing.

Competent authorities—their powers and resources

Recommendation Twenty-six

Countries should establish an FIU that serves as a national centre for the receiving (and, as permitted, requesting), analysis, and dissemination of STR and other information regarding potential money laundering or terrorist financing. The FIU should have access, directly or indirectly, on a timely basis to the financial, administrative, and law enforcement information that it requires to properly undertake its functions, including the analysis of STR.

Recommendation Twenty-seven
Countries should ensure that designated law enforcement authorities have responsibility for money laundering and terrorist financing investigations. Countries are encouraged to support and develop, as far as possible, special investigative techniques suitable for the investigation of money laundering, such as controlled delivery, undercover operations, and other relevant techniques. Countries are also encouraged to use other effective mechanisms such as the use of permanent or temporary groups specialized in asset investigation and co-operative investigations with appropriate competent authorities in other countries.

Recommendation Twenty-eight
When conducting investigations of money laundering and underlying predicate offences, competent authorities should be able to obtain documents and information for use in those investigations and in prosecutions and related actions. This should include powers to use compulsory measures for the production of records held by financial institutions and other persons, for the search of persons and premises, and for the seizure and obtaining of evidence.

Recommendation Twenty-nine
Supervisors should have adequate powers to monitor and ensure compliance by financial institutions with requirements to combat money laundering and terrorist financing, including the authority to conduct inspections. They should be authorised to compel production of any information from financial institutions that is relevant to monitoring such compliance and to impose adequate administrative sanctions for failure to comply with such requirements.

Recommendation Thirty
Countries should provide their competent authorities involved in combating money laundering and terrorist financing with adequate financial, human, and technical resources. Countries should have in place processes to ensure that the staffs of those authorities are of high integrity.

Recommendation Thirty-one

Countries should ensure that policy makers, the FIU, law enforcement, and supervisors have effective mechanisms in place which enable them to co-operate, and where appropriate, coordinate domestically with each other concerning the development and implementation of policies and activities to combat money laundering and terrorist financing.

Recommendation Thirty-two

Countries should ensure that their competent authorities could review the effectiveness of their systems to combat money laundering and terrorist financing systems by maintaining comprehensive statistics on matters relevant to the effectiveness and efficiency of such systems. This should include statistics on the STR received and disseminated on money laundering and terrorist financing investigations, prosecutions, and convictions; on property frozen, seized and confiscated; and on mutual legal assistance or other international requests for co-operation.

Transparency of legal persons and arrangements

Recommendation Thirty-three

Countries should take measures to prevent the unlawful use of legal persons by money launderers. Countries should ensure that there is adequate, accurate, and timely information on the beneficial ownership and control of legal persons that can be obtained or accessed in a timely fashion by competent authorities. In particular, countries that have legal persons who are able to issue bearer shares should take appropriate measures to ensure they are not misused for money laundering and be able to demonstrate the adequacy of those measures. Countries could consider measures to facilitate access to beneficial ownership and control information to financial institutions undertaking the requirements set out in five.

Recommendation Thirty-four

Countries should take measures to prevent the unlawful use of legal arrangements by money launderers. In particular, countries

227

should ensure that there is adequate, accurate, and timely information on express trusts, including information on the settlor, trustee, and beneficiaries that can be obtained or accessed in a timely fashion by competent authorities. Countries could consider measures to facilitate access to beneficial ownership and control information to financial institutions undertaking the requirements set out in five.

International cooperation

Recommendation Thirty-five
Countries should take immediate steps to become party to and implement fully the Vienna Convention, the Palermo Convention, and the 1999 United Nations International Convention for the Suppression of the Financing of Terrorism. Countries are also encouraged to ratify and implement other relevant international conventions, such as the 1990 Council of Europe Convention on Laundering, Search, Seizure, and Confiscation of the Proceeds from Crime and the 2002 Inter-American Convention against Terrorism.

Mutual legal assistance and extradition

Recommendation Thirty-six
Countries should rapidly, constructively, and effectively provide the widest possible range of mutual legal assistance in relation to money laundering and terrorist financing investigations, prosecutions, and related proceedings. In particular, countries should:

a) Not prohibit or place unreasonable or unduly restrictive conditions on the provision of mutual legal assistance.
b) Ensure they have clear and efficient processes for the execution of mutual legal assistance requests.
c) Not refuse to execute a request for mutual legal assistance on the sole ground that the offence is also considered to involve fiscal matters.

d) Not refuse to execute a request for mutual legal assistance on the grounds that laws require financial institutions to maintain secrecy or confidentiality.

Countries should ensure that the powers of their competent authorities required under Recommendation twenty-eight are also available for use in response to requests for mutual legal assistance and if consistent with their domestic framework, in response to direct requests from foreign judicial or law enforcement authorities to domestic counterparts.

To avoid conflicts of jurisdiction, consideration should be given to devising and applying mechanisms for determining the best venue for prosecution of defendants in the interests of justice in cases that are subject to prosecution in more than one country.

Recommendation Thirty-seven
Countries should, to the greatest extent possible, render mutual legal assistance notwithstanding the absence of dual criminality.

Where dual criminality is required for mutual legal assistance or extradition, that requirement should be deemed to be satisfied regardless of whether both countries place the offence within the same category of offence or denominate the offence by the same terminology provided that both countries criminalize the conduct underlying the offence.

Recommendation Thirty-eight
There should be authority to take expeditious action in response to requests by foreign countries to identify, freeze, seize and confiscate property laundered, proceeds from money laundering or predicate offences, instrumentalities used in or intended for use in the commission of these offences, or property of corresponding value. There should also be arrangements for coordinating seizure and confiscation proceedings, which may include the sharing of confiscated assets.

Recommendation Thirty-nine

Countries should recognize money laundering as an extraditable offence. Each country should extradite its own nationals, or where a country does not do so solely on the grounds of nationality, that country should, at the request of the country seeking extradition, submit the case without undue delay to its competent authorities for the purpose of prosecution of the offences set forth in the request. Those authorities should take their decision and conduct their proceedings in the same manner as in the case of any other offence of a serious nature under the domestic law of that country. The countries concerned should cooperate with each other, in particular, on procedural and evidentiary aspects, to ensure the efficiency of such prosecutions.

Subject to their legal frameworks, countries may consider simplifying extradition by allowing direct transmission of extradition requests between appropriate ministries, extraditing persons based only on warrants of arrests or judgments, and/or introducing a simplified extradition of consenting persons who waive formal extradition proceedings.

Other forms of cooperation

Recommendation Forty

Countries should ensure that their competent authorities provide the widest possible range of international co-operation to their foreign counterparts. There should be clear and effective gateways to facilitate the prompt and constructive exchange directly between counterparts, either spontaneously or upon request, of information relating to both money laundering and the underlying predicate offences. Exchanges should be permitted without unduly restrictive conditions. In particular:

a) Competent authorities should not refuse a request for assistance on the sole ground that the request is also considered to involve fiscal matters.

b) Countries should not invoke laws that require financial institutions to maintain secrecy or confidentiality as a ground for refusing to provide co-operation.

c) Competent authorities should be able to conduct inquiries; and where possible, investigations on behalf of foreign counterparts.

Where the ability to obtain information sought by a foreign competent authority is not within the mandate of its counterpart, countries are also encouraged to permit a prompt and constructive exchange of information with non-counterparts. Cooperation with foreign authorities other than counterparts could occur directly or indirectly. When uncertain about the appropriate avenue to follow, competent authorities should first contact their foreign counterparts for assistance.

Countries should establish controls and safeguards to ensure that information exchanged by competent authorities is used only in an authorized manner, consistent with their obligations concerning privacy and data protection.

The Interpretative Notes

General information
Reference in this document to "countries" should be taken to apply equally to "territories" or "jurisdictions."

Recommendations five to sixteen and twenty-one to twenty-two state that financial institutions or designated non-financial businesses and professions should take certain actions. These references require countries to take measures that will oblige financial institutions or designated non-financial businesses and professions to comply with each recommendation. The basic obligations under Recommendations five, ten, and thirteen should be set out in law or regulation, while more detailed elements in those recommendations, as well as obligations under other recommendations, could be required either by law or regulation or by other enforceable means issued by a competent authority.

Where reference is made to a financial institution being satisfied as to a matter, that institution must be able to justify its assessment to competent authorities.
To comply with Recommendations twelve and sixteen, countries do not need to issue laws or regulations that relate exclusively to lawyers, notaries, accountants, and the other designated non-financial businesses and professions so long as these businesses or professions are included in laws or regulations covering the underlying activities.

The Interpretative Notes that apply to financial institutions are also relevant to designated non-financial businesses and professions, where applicable.
Interpretative Note to Recommendations five, twelve, and sixteen

The designated thresholds for transactions (under Recommendations five and twelve) are as follows:

a. Financial institutions (for occasional customers under Recommendation five) - USD/EUR 15,000.
b. Casinos, including internet casinos (under Recommendation twelve) - USD/EUR 3000.
c. For dealers in precious metals and dealers in precious stones when engaged in any cash transaction (under Recommendations twelve and sixteen) - USD/EUR 15,000.
d. Financial transactions above a designated threshold include situations when the transaction is carried out in a single operation or in several operations that appear to be linked.

(See Recommendations five, twelve, and sixteen)

Interpretative Note to Recommendation five (Thresholds Interpretative Note)

Customer due diligence and tipping off
1. If, during the establishment or course of the customer relationship, or when conducting occasional transactions, a financial institution suspects that transactions relate to money laundering or terrorist financing, then the institution should:

a) Normally seek to identify and verify the identity of the customer and the beneficial owner, whether permanent or occasional, and irrespective of any exemption or any designated threshold that might otherwise apply.
b) Make an STR to the FIU in accordance with Recommendation thirteen.

2. Recommendation fourteen prohibits financial institutions, their directors, officers, and employees from disclosing the fact that an STR or related information is being reported to the FIU. A risk exists that customers could be unintentionally tipped off when the financial institution is seeking to perform its customer due diligence (CDD) obligations in these circumstances. The customer's awareness of a possible STR or investigation could com-

promise future efforts to investigate the suspected money laundering or terrorist financing operation.

3. Therefore, if financial institutions form a suspicion that transactions relate to money laundering or terrorist financing, they should take into account the risk of tipping off when performing the customer due diligence process. If the institution reasonably believes that performing the CDD process will tip-off the customer or potential customer, it may choose not to pursue that process and should file an STR. Institutions should ensure that their employees are aware of and sensitive to these issues when conducting CDD.

CDD for legal persons and arrangements:

4. When performing elements (a) and (b) of the CDD process in relation to legal persons or arrangements, financial institutions should:

a) Verify that any person purporting to act on behalf of the customer is so authorized and identify that person.
b) Identify the customer and verify its identity the types of measures that would be normally needed to satisfactorily perform this function would require obtaining proof of incorporation or similar evidence of the legal status of the legal person or arrangement, as well as information concerning the customer's name, the names of trustees, legal form, address, directors, and provisions regulating the power to bind the legal person or arrangement.
c) Identify the beneficial owners, including forming and understanding of the ownership and control structure, and take reasonable measures to verify the identity of such persons. The types of measures that would be normally needed to satisfactorily perform this function would require identifying the natural persons with a controlling interest and identifying the natural persons who comprise the mind and management of the legal person or arrangement. Where the customer or the owner of the controlling interest is a public company that is

subject to regulatory disclosure requirements, it is not necessary to seek to identify and verify the identity of any shareholder of that company.

The relevant information or data may be obtained from a public register from the customer or from other reliable sources.

Reliance on identification and verification already performed:

5. The CDD measures set out in Recommendation five do not imply that financial institutions have to repeatedly identify and verify the identity of each customer every time that a customer conducts a transaction. An institution is entitled to rely on the identification and verification steps that it has already undertaken unless it has doubts about the veracity of that information. Examples of situations that might lead an institution to have such doubts could be where there is a suspicion of money laundering in relation to that customer, or where there is a material change in the way the customer's account is operated which is not consistent with the customer's business profile.

Timing of verification:

6. Examples of the types of circumstances where it would be permissible for verification to be completed after the establishment of the business relationship because it would be essential not to interrupt the normal conduct of business include:

a. Non face-to-face business
Securities transactions. In the securities industry, companies and intermediaries may be required to perform transactions very rapidly, according to the market conditions at the time the customer is contacting them, and the performance of the transaction may be required before verification of identity is completed.
c. Life insurance business. In relation to life insurance business, countries may permit the identification and verification of the beneficiary under the policy to take place after having established the business relationship with the policyholder. However,

in all such cases, identification and verification should occur at or before the time of payout or the time where the beneficiary intends to exercise vested rights under the policy.

7. Financial institutions will also need to adopt risk management procedures with respect to the conditions under which a customer may utilise the business relationship prior to verification. These procedures should include a set of measures such as a limitation of the number, types and/or amount of transactions that can be performed and the monitoring of large or complex transactions being carried out outside of expected norms for that type of relationship. Financial institutions should refer to the Basel CDD paper (section 2.2.6.) (*Guidance Paper on Customer Due Diligence for Banks* issued by the Basel Committee on Banking Supervision in October 2001) for specific guidance on examples of risk management measures for non-face to face business.

Requirement to identify existing customers
8. The principles set out in the Basel CDD paper concerning the identification of existing customers should serve as guidance when applying customer due diligence processes to institutions engaged in banking activity and could apply to other financial institutions where relevant.

Simplified or reduced CDD measures
9. The general rule is that customers must be subject to the full range of CDD measures, including the requirement to identify the beneficial owner. Nevertheless, there are circumstances where the risk of money laundering or terrorist financing is lower, where information on the identity of the customer and the beneficial owner of a customer is publicly available, or where adequate checks and controls exist elsewhere in national systems. In such circumstances, it could be reasonable for a country to allow its financial institutions to apply simplified or reduced CDD measures when identifying and verifying the identity of the customer and the beneficial owner.

10. Examples of customers where simplified or reduced CDD measures could apply are:

Financial institutions: where they are subject to requirements to combat money laundering and terrorist financing consistent with the FATF Recommendations and are supervised for compliance with those controls.
   a. Public companies that are subject to regulatory disclosure requirements
   b. Government administrations or enterprises

11. Simplified or reduced CDD measures could also apply to the beneficial owners of pooled accounts held by designated non-financial businesses or professions provided that those businesses or professions are subject to requirements to combat money laundering and terrorist financing consistent with the FATF Recommendations and are subject to effective systems for monitoring and ensuring their compliance with those requirements. Banks should also refer to the Basel CDD paper (section 2.2.4.), which provides specific guidance concerning situations where an account holding institution may rely on a customer that is a professional financial intermediary to perform the customer due diligence on his or its own customers (i.e. the beneficial owners of the bank account). Where relevant, the CDD Paper could also provide guidance in relation to similar accounts held by other types of financial institutions.

12. Simplified CDD or reduced measures could also be acceptable for various types of products or transactions such as (examples only):

   a. Life insurance policies where the annual premium is no more than USD/EUR 1000 or a single premium of no more than USD/EUR 2500
   b. Insurance policies for pension schemes if there is no surrender clause, and the policy cannot be used as collateral

A pension, superannuation, or similar scheme that provides retirement benefits to employees, where contributions are made by way of deduction from wages and the scheme rules do not permit the assignment of a member's interest under the scheme.

13. Countries could also decide whether financial institutions could apply these simplified measures only to customers in its own jurisdiction or allow them to do for customers from any other jurisdiction that the original country is satisfied is in compliance with and has effectively implemented the FATF Recommendations.

Simplified CDD measures are not acceptable whenever there is suspicion of money laundering or terrorist financing or specific higher risk scenarios apply.

(See Recommendation five)

Interpretative Note to Recommendation Six
Countries are encouraged to extend the requirements of Recommendation six to individuals who hold prominent public functions in their own country.

(See Recommendation six)

Interpretative Note to Recommendation nine
This recommendation does not apply to outsourcing or agency relationships.

This recommendation also does not apply to relationships, accounts, or transactions between financial institutions for their clients. Those relationships are addressed by Recommendations five and seven.

(See Recommendation nine)

Interpretative Note to Recommendation ten and eleven

In relation to insurance business, the word "transactions" should be understood to refer to the insurance product itself, the premium payment, and the benefits.

(See Recommendation ten and Recommendation eleven)

Interpretative Note to Recommendation twelve
The designated thresholds for transactions (under Recommendations five and twelve) are as follows:

   a. Financial institutions (for occasional customers under Recommendation five) - USD/EUR 15,000
   b. Casinos, including internet casinos (under Recommendation twelve) - USD/EUR 3000
   c. For dealers in precious metals and dealers in precious stones when engaged in any cash transaction (under Recommendations twelve and sixteen) - USD/EUR 15,000

Financial transactions above a designated threshold include situations where the transaction is carried out in a single operation or in several operations that appear to be linked
(See Recommendation twelve)

Interpretative Note to Recommendation thirteen

The reference to criminal activity in Recommendation thirteen refers to:
a) all criminal acts that would constitute a predicate offence for money laundering in the jurisdiction; or
b) at a minimum, to those offences that would constitute a predicate offence as required by Recommendation one

Countries are strongly encouraged to adopt alternative (a). All suspicious transactions, including attempted transactions, should be reported regardless of the amount of the transaction.

In implementing Recommendation thirteen, suspicious transactions should be reported by financial institutions regardless of whether they are also thought to involve tax matters. Countries should take into account that, in order to deter financial institutions from reporting a suspicious transaction, money launderers may seek to state, *inter alia,* that their transactions relate to tax matters.

(See Recommendation thirteen)

Interpretative Note to Recommendation fourteen(tipping off)
Where lawyers, notaries, other independent legal professionals, and accountants acting as independent legal professionals seek to dissuade a client from engaging in illegal activity, this does not amount to tipping off.

(See Recommendation fourteen)

Interpretative Note to Recommendation fifteen
The type and extent of measures to be taken for each of the requirements set out in the Recommendation should be appropriate, having regard to the risk of money laundering and terrorist financing and the size of the business.

For financial institutions, compliance management arrangements should include the appointment of a compliance officer at the management level.

(See Recommendation fifteen)

Interpretative Note to Recommendation sixteen (Thresholds Interpretative Note)

1. It is for each jurisdiction to determine the matters that would fall under legal professional privilege or professional secrecy. This would normally cover information lawyers, notaries, or other independent legal professionals receive from or obtain through one of their clients:

(a) in the course of ascertaining the legal position of their client, or

(b) in performing their task of defending or representing that client in, or concerning judicial, administrative, arbitration, or mediation proceedings. Where accountants are subject to the same obligations of secrecy or privilege, then they are also not required to report suspicious transactions.

2. Countries may allow lawyers, notaries, other independent legal professionals, and accountants to send their STR to their appropriate self-regulatory organizations, provided that there are appropriate forms of co-operation between these organizations and the FIU.

(See Recommendation sixteen)

Interpretative Note to Recommendation nineteen
(Recommendation deleted 22 October 2004)

(See Recommendation nineteen)

Interpretative Note to Recommendation twenty-three
Recommendation twenty-three should not be read as to require the introduction of a system of regular review of licensing of controlling interests in financial institutions merely for anti-money laundering purposes but as to stress the desirability of suitability review for controlling shareholders in financial institutions (banks and non-banks in particular) from a FATF point of view. Hence, where shareholder suitability (or "fit and proper") tests exist, the attention of supervisors should be drawn to their relevance for anti-money laundering purposes.

(See Recommendation twenty-three)

Interpretative Note to Recommendation twenty-five
When considering the feedback that should be provided, countries should have regard to the FATF Best Practice Guidelines on

Providing Feedback to Reporting Financial Institutions and Other Persons.

(See Recommendation twenty-five)

Interpretative Note to Recommendation twenty-six
Where a country has created an FIU, it should consider applying for membership in the Egmont Group. Countries should have regard to the Egmont Group Statement of Purpose, and its Principles for Information Exchange between Financial Intelligence Units for Money Laundering Cases. These documents set out important guidance concerning the role and functions of FIUs and the mechanisms for exchanging information between FIU.

(See Recommendation twenty-six)

Interpretative Note to Recommendation twenty-seven
Countries should consider taking measures, including legislative ones, at the national level, to allow their competent authorities investigating money laundering cases to postpone or waive the arrest of suspected persons and or the seizure of the money for the purpose of identifying persons involved in such activities or for evidence gathering. Without such measures, the use of procedures such as controlled deliveries and undercover operations are precluded.

(See Recommendation twenty-seven)

Interpretative Note to Recommendation thirty-eight
Countries should consider:

a) Establishing an asset forfeiture fund in its respective country into which all or a portion of confiscated property will be deposited for law enforcement, health, education, or other appropriate purposes;
b) Taking such measures as may be necessary to enable it to share among or between other countries confiscated property, in

particular, when confiscation is directly or indirectly a result of coordinated law enforcement actions

(See Recommendation thirty-eight)

Interpretative Note to Recommendation forty

1. For the purposes of this recommendation:

"Counterparts" refers to authorities who exercise similar responsibilities and functions.
"Competent authority" refers to all administrative and law enforcement authorities concerned with combating money laundering and terrorist financing, including the FIU and supervisors.

2. Depending on the type of competent authority involved and the nature and purpose of the co-operation, different channels can be appropriate for the exchange of information. Examples of mechanisms or channels that are used to exchange information include: bilateral or multilateral agreements or arrangements, memoranda of understanding, exchanges on the basis of reciprocity, or through appropriate international or regional organizations. However, this recommendation is not intended to cover cooperation in relation to mutual legal assistance or extradition.
3. The reference to indirect exchange of information with foreign authorities other than counterparts covers the situation where the requested information passes from the foreign authority through one or more domestic or foreign authorities before being received by the requesting authority. The competent authority that requests the information should always make it clear for what purpose and on whose behalf the request is made.
4. FIUs should be able to make inquiries on behalf of foreign counterparts where this could be relevant to an analysis of financial transactions. At a minimum, inquiries should include:

- Searching its own databases, which would include information related to suspicious transaction reports.

- Searching other databases to which it may have direct or indirect access, including law enforcement databases, public databases, administrative databases, and commercially available databases.
- Where permitted to do so, FIUs should also contact other competent authorities and financial institutions in order to obtain relevant information.

Nine Special Recommendations (SR) on Terrorist Financing (TF)

Please note: the Special Recommendations numbered eight until 22 October 2004, when the ninth was adopted by the Plenary.
Interpretative Notes to the Special Recommendations
International Best Practices print versions
FATF Forty Recommendations (2003)

I. Ratification and implementation of United Nations instruments
II. Criminalizing the financing of terrorism and associated money laundering
III. Freezing and confiscating terrorist assets
IV. Reporting suspicious transactions related to terrorism
V. International cooperation
VI. Alternative remittance
VII. Wire transfers
VIII. Non-profit organizations
IX. Cash couriers

Recognizing the vital importance of taking action to combat the financing of terrorism, the FATF has agreed these recommendations, which, when combined with the FATF Forty Recommendations on money laundering, set out the basic framework to detect, prevent, and suppress the financing of terrorism and terrorist acts. For further information on the Special Recommendations as related to the self-assessment process, see the Guidance Notes.

I. Ratification and implementation of United Nations instruments

Each country should take immediate steps to ratify and to implement fully the 1999 United Nations International Convention for the Suppression of the Financing of Terrorism.

Countries should also immediately implement the United Nations resolutions relating to the prevention and suppression of the financing of terrorist acts, particularly United Nations Security Council Resolution 1373.

II. Criminalizing the financing of terrorism and associated money laundering

Each country should criminalize the financing of terrorism, terrorist acts, and terrorist organizations. Countries should ensure that such offences are designated as money laundering predicate offences.

III. Freezing and confiscating terrorist assets

Each country should implement measures to freeze without delay funds or other assets of terrorists, those who finance terrorism, and terrorist organizations in accordance with the United Nations resolutions relating to the prevention and suppression of the financing of terrorist acts.

Each country should also adopt and implement measures, including legislative ones, which would enable the competent authorities to seize and confiscate property that is the proceeds of, or used in, or intended or allocated for use in, the financing of terrorism, terrorist acts, or terrorist organizations.

IV. Reporting suspicious transactions related to terrorism

If financial institutions or other businesses or entities subject to anti-money laundering obligations suspect or have reasonable grounds to suspect that funds are linked or related to or are to be used for terrorism, terrorist acts, or by terrorist organizations, they should be required to report promptly their suspicions to the competent authorities.

V. International co-operation

Each country should afford another country, on the basis of a treaty, arrangement, or other mechanism for mutual legal assistance or information exchange, the greatest possible measure of assistance in connection with criminal, civil enforcement, and administrative investigations, inquiries, and proceedings relating to the financing of terrorism, terrorist acts, and terrorist organizations.

Countries should also take all possible measures to ensure that they do not provide safe havens for individuals charged with the financing of terrorism, terrorist acts, or terrorist organizations, and should have procedures in place to extradite, where possible, such individuals.

VI. Alternative remittance

Each country should take measures to ensure that persons or legal entities, including agents, that provide a service for the transmission of money or value, including transmission through an informal money or value transfer system or network, should be licensed or registered and subject to all the FATF Recommendations that apply to banks and non-bank financial institutions. Each country should ensure that persons or legal entities that carry out this service illegally are subject to administrative, civil, or criminal sanctions.

VII. Wire transfers

Countries should take measures to require financial institutions, including money remitters, to include accurate and meaningful originator information (name, address, and account number) on funds transfers and related messages that are sent, and the information should remain with the transfer or related message through the payment chain.

Countries should take measures to ensure that financial institutions, including money remitters, conduct enhanced scrutiny of and monitor for suspicious activity funds transfers which do not contain complete originator information (name, address and account number).

VIII. Non-profit organizations

Countries should review the adequacy of laws and regulations that relate to entities that can be abused for the financing of terrorism. Non-profit organizations are particularly vulnerable, and countries should ensure that they cannot be misused:

- by terrorist organizations posing as legitimate entities;
- to exploit legitimate entities as conduits for terrorist financing, including for the purpose of escaping asset freezing measures and;
- to conceal or obscure the clandestine diversion of funds intended for legitimate purposes to terrorist organizations.

IX. Cash couriers

Countries should have measures in place to detect the physical cross-border transportation of currency and bearer negotiable instruments, including a declaration system or other disclosure obligation.

Countries should ensure that their competent authorities have the legal authority to stop or restrain currency or bearer negotiable instruments that are suspected to be related to terrorist financing or money laundering, or that are falsely declared or disclosed.

Countries should ensure that effective, proportionate, and dissuasive sanctions are available to deal with persons who make false declaration(s) or disclosure(s). In cases where the currency or bearer negotiable instruments are related to terrorist financing or money laundering, countries should also adopt measures, including legislative ones consistent with Recommendation three and Special Recommendation III, which would enable the confiscation of such currency or instruments.

Note:
With the adoption of Special Recommendation IX, the FATF now deletes paragraph nineteen (a) of Recommendation nineteen and the Interpretative Note to Recommendation nineteen in order to ensure internal consistency amongst the FATF Recommendations. The modified text of recommendation nineteen reads as follows:

Recommendation nineteen
Countries should consider the feasibility and utility of a system where banks and other financial institutions and intermediaries would report all domestic and international currency transactions above a fixed amount to a national central agency with a computerized data base available to competent authorities for use in money laundering or terrorist financing cases subject to strict safeguards to ensure proper use of the information.

Interpretative Notes to the Nine Special Recommendations

Interpretative Note to Special Recommendation II: Criminalizing the financing of terrorism and associated money laundering

Objective
Special Recommendation II was developed with the objective of ensuring that countries have the legal capacity to prosecute and apply criminal sanctions to persons who finance terrorism. Given the close connection between international terrorism and *inter alia,* money laundering, another objective of Special Recommendation II is to emphasize this link by obligating countries to include terrorist financing offences as predicate offences for money laundering. The basis for criminalizing terrorist financing should be the United Nations International Convention for the Suppression of the Financing of Terrorism 1999 [1].

Definitions
For the purposes of the Special Recommendation II and this Interpretative Note, the following definitions apply:
The term "funds" refers to assets of every kind, whether tangible or intangible, movable or immovable, however acquired, and legal documents or instruments in any form, including electronic or digital, evidencing title to, or interest in, such assets, including, but not limited to, bank credits, traveller's cheques, bank cheques, money orders, shares, securities, bonds, drafts, and letters of credit.

The term "terrorist" refers to any natural person who:
(I)   commits or attempts to commit terrorist acts by any means, directly or indirectly, unlawfully and willfully;
(ii)   participates as an accomplice in terrorist acts;
(iii) organizes or directs others to commit terrorist acts or;
(iv)   contributes to the commission of terrorist acts by a group of persons acting with a common purpose where the contribution is made intentionally and with the aim of fur-

thering the terrorist act or with the knowledge of the intention of the group to commit a terrorist act.

The term "terrorist act" includes:

(I)   An act which constitutes an offence within the scope of, and as defined in one of the following treaties: Convention for the Suppression of Unlawful Seizure of Aircraft (1970), Convention for the Suppression of Unlawful Acts against the Safety of Civil Aviation (1971), Convention on the Prevention and Punishment of Crimes against Internationally Protected Persons, including Diplomatic Agents (1973), International Convention against the Taking of Hostages (1979), Convention on the Physical Protection of Nuclear Material (1980), Protocol for the Suppression of Unlawful Acts of Violence at Airports Serving International Civil Aviation, supplementary to the Convention for the Suppression of Unlawful Acts against the Safety of Civil Aviation (1988), Convention for the Suppression of Unlawful Acts against the Safety of Maritime Navigation (1988), Protocol for the Suppression of Unlawful Acts against the Safety of Fixed Platforms located on the Continental Shelf (1988), and the International Convention for the Suppression of Terrorist Bombings (1997) and;

(ii) Any other act intended to cause death or serious bodily injury to a civilian or to any other person not taking an active part in the hostilities in a situation of armed conflict when the purpose of such act, by its nature or context, is to intimidate a population or to compel a government or an international organization to do or to abstain from doing any act.

The term "terrorist financing" includes the financing of terrorist acts and of terrorists and terrorist organizations.

The term "terrorist organization" refers to any group of terrorists that:

(i)   commits or attempts to commit terrorist acts by any means, directly or indirectly, unlawfully and willfully;

(ii)   participates as an accomplice in terrorist acts;
(iii) organizes or directs others to commit terrorist acts; or
(iv)   contributes to the commission of terrorist acts by a group
       of persons acting with a common purpose where the con-
       tribution is made intentionally and with the aim of fur-
       thering the terrorist act or with the knowledge of the
       intention of the group to commit a terrorist act.

Characteristics of the Terrorist Financing Offence
Terrorist financing offences should extend to any person who
willfully provides or collects funds by any means, directly or indirectly, with the unlawful intention that they should be used or
in the knowledge that they are to be used, in full or in part:
(a) to carry out a terrorist act(s);
(b) by a terrorist organization; or
(c) by an individual terrorist.

Criminalizing terrorist financing solely on the basis of aiding and
abetting, attempt, or conspiracy does not comply with this recommendation.

Terrorist financing offences should extend to any funds whether
from a legitimate or illegitimate source.
Terrorist financing offences should not require that the funds:
(a) were actually used to carry out or attempt a terrorist act(s); or
(b) be linked to a specific terrorist act(s).

It should also be an offence to attempt to commit the offence of
terrorist financing.

It should also be an offence to engage in any of the following
types of conduct:
a. Participating as an accomplice in an offence as set forth in paragraphs three or seven of this Interpretative Note;
b. Organizing or directing others to commit an offence as set
forth in paragraphs three or seven of this Interpretative Note;
Contributing to the commission of one or more offence(s) as set
forth in paragraphs three or seven of this Interpretative Note by

a group of persons acting with a common purpose. Such contribution shall be intentional and shall either:

(i) be made with the aim of furthering the criminal activity or criminal purpose of the group, where such activity or purpose involves the commission of a terrorist financing offence; or

(ii) be made in the knowledge of the intention of the group to commit a terrorist financing offence.

Terrorist financing offences should be predicate offences for money laundering.

Terrorist financing offences should apply, regardless of whether the person alleged to have committed the offence(s) is in the same country or a different country from the one in which the terrorist(s) or terrorist organization(s) is located or the terrorist act(s) occurred or will occur.

The law should permit the intentional element of the terrorist financing offence to be inferred from objective factual circumstances.

Criminal liability for terrorist financing should extend to legal persons. Where that is not possible (i.e. due to fundamental principles of domestic law), civil or administrative liability should apply.

Making legal persons subject to criminal liability for terrorist financing should not preclude the possibility of parallel criminal, civil, or administrative proceedings in countries in which more than one form of liability is available.

Natural and legal persons should be subject to effective, proportionate, and dissuasive criminal, civil, or administrative, sanctions for terrorist financing.

Footnotes:

Although the United Nations Convention had not yet come into force at the time that Special Recommendation II was originally issued in October 2001—and thus is not cited in the Special Recommendation itself—the intent of the FATF has been from the issuance of Special Recommendation II to reiterate and reinforce the criminalization standard as set forth in the convention (in particular, article two). The convention came into force in April 2003.

Interpretative Note to Special Recommendation III: Freezing and Confiscating Terrorist Assets

Objectives

FATF Special Recommendation III consists of two obligations. The first requires jurisdictions to implement measures that will freeze or, if appropriate, seize terrorist related funds or other assets without delay in accordance with relevant United Nations resolutions. The second obligation of Special Recommendation III is to have measures in place that permit a jurisdiction to seize or confiscate terrorist funds or other assets on the basis of an order or mechanism issued by a competent authority or a court.

The objective of the first requirement is to freeze terrorist related funds or other assets based on reasonable grounds, or a reasonable basis, to suspect or believe that such funds or other assets could be used to finance terrorist activity. The objective of the second requirement is to deprive terrorists of these funds or other assets if and when links have been adequately established between the funds or other assets and terrorists or terrorist activity. The intent of the first objective is preventative, while the intent of the second objective is mainly preventative and punitive. Both requirements are necessary to deprive terrorists and terrorist networks of the means to conduct future terrorist activity and maintain their infrastructure and operations.

Scope

Special Recommendation III is intended, with regard to its first requirement, to complement the obligations in the context of the United Nations Security Council (UNSC) resolutions relating to the prevention and suppression of the financing of terrorist acts— S/RES/1267(1999) and its successor resolutions [1] S/RES/1373(2001) and any prospective resolutions related to the freezing, or if appropriate, seizure of terrorist assets. It should be stressed that none of the obligations in Special Recommendation III is intended to replace other measures or obligations that may already be in place for dealing with funds or other assets in the context of a criminal, civil, or administrative, investigation or proceeding [2]. The focus of Special Recommendation III, instead, is on the preventative measures that are necessary and unique in the context of stopping the flow or use of funds or other assets to terrorist groups.

S/RES/1267(1999) and S/RES/1373(2001) differ in the persons and entities whose funds or other assets are to be frozen, the authorities responsible for making these designations, and the effect of these designations.

S/RES/1267(1999) and its successor resolutions obligate jurisdictions to freeze without delay the funds or other assets owned or controlled by Al-Qaida, the Taliban, Usama bin Laden, or persons and entities associated with them as designated by the United Nations Al-Qaida and Taliban Sanctions Committee established pursuant to United Nations Security Council Resolution 1267 (the Al-Qaida and Taliban Sanctions Committee), including funds derived from funds or other assets owned or controlled, directly or indirectly, by them or by persons acting on their behalf or at their direction and ensure that neither these nor any other funds or other assets are made available, directly or indirectly, for such persons' benefit, by their nationals or by any person within their territory. The Al-Qaida and Taliban Sanctions Committee is the authority responsible for designating the persons and entities that should have their funds or other assets frozen under S/RES/1267(1999). All jurisdictions that are members of the United Nations are obligated by S/RES/1267(1999) to freeze the assets of persons and entities so designated by the Al-Qaida and Taliban Sanctions Committee. [3]

S/RES/1373(2001) obligates jurisdictions [4] to freeze without delay the funds or other assets of persons who commit, or attempt to commit, terrorist acts or participate in or facilitate the commission of terrorist acts; of entities owned or controlled directly or indirectly by such persons; and of persons and entities acting on behalf of, or at the direction of such persons and entities, including funds or other assets derived or generated from property owned or controlled, directly or indirectly, by such persons and associated persons and entities. Each individual jurisdiction has the authority to designate the persons and entities that should have their funds or other assets frozen. Additionally, to ensure that effective co-operation is developed among jurisdictions, jurisdictions should examine and give effect to, if appropriate, the actions initiated under the freezing mechanisms of other jurisdictions. When (i) a specific notification or communication is sent and (ii) the jurisdiction receiving the request is satisfied, according to applicable legal principles, that a requested designation is supported by reasonable grounds or a reasonable basis to suspect or believe that the proposed designee is a terrorist, one who finances terrorism or a terrorist organization, the jurisdiction receiving the request must ensure that the funds or other assets of the designated person are frozen without delay.

Definitions

For the purposes of Special Recommendation III and this Interpretive Note, the following definitions apply:

The term "freeze" means to prohibit the transfer, conversion, disposition, or movement of funds or other assets on the basis of, and for the duration of the validity of, an action initiated by a competent authority or a court under a freezing mechanism. The frozen funds or other assets remain the property of the person(s) or entity(ies) that held an interest in the specified funds or other assets at the time of the freezing and may continue to be administered by the financial institution or other arrangements designated by such person(s) or entity prior to the initiation of an action under a freezing mechanism.

The term "seize" means to prohibit the transfer, conversion, disposition, or movement of funds or other assets on the basis of an action initiated by a competent authority or a court under a freezing mechanism. However, unlike a freezing action, a seizure is effected by a mechanism that allows the competent authority or court to take control of specified funds or other assets. The seized funds or other assets remain the property of the person(s) or entity that held an interest in the specified funds or other assets at the time of the seizure, although the competent authority or court will often take over possession, administration, or management of the seized funds or other assets.

The term "confiscate," which includes forfeiture where applicable, means the permanent deprivation of funds or other assets by order of a competent authority or a court. Confiscation or forfeiture takes place through a judicial or administrative procedure that transfers the ownership of specified funds or other assets to be transferred to the state. In this case, the person(s) or entity(ies) that held an interest in the specified funds or other assets at the time of the confiscation or forfeiture loses all rights, in principle, to the confiscated or forfeited funds or other assets. [5]

The term "funds or other assets" means financial assets, property of every kind, whether tangible or intangible, movable or immovable, however acquired, and legal documents or instruments in any form, including electronic or digital, evidencing title to, or interest in, such funds or other assets, including, but not limited to, bank credits, traveller's cheques, bank cheques, money orders, shares, securities, bonds, drafts, or letters of credit, and any interest, dividends or other income on or value accruing from or generated by such funds or other assets.

The term "terrorist" refers to any natural person who:
(I) commits, or attempts to commit, terrorist acts [6] by any means, directly or indirectly, unlawfully and willfully;
(ii) participates as an accomplice in terrorist acts or terrorist financing;
(iii) organizes or directs others to commit terrorist acts or terrorist financing; or
(iv) contributes to the commission of terrorist acts or terrorist financing by a group of persons acting with a common purpose where the contribution is made intentionally and with the aim of furthering the terrorist act or terrorist financing or with the knowledge of the intention of the group to commit a terrorist act or terrorist financing.

The phrase "those who finance terrorism" refers to any person, group, undertaking, or other entity that provides or collects, by any means, directly or indirectly, funds or other assets that may be used, in full or in part, to facilitate the commission of terrorist acts, or to any persons or entities acting on behalf of or at the direction of such persons, groups, undertakings or other entities. This includes those who provide or collect funds or other assets with the intention that they should be used or in the knowledge that they are to be used, in full or in part, in order to carry out terrorist acts.

The term "terrorist organization" refers to any legal person, group, undertaking, or other entity owned or controlled, directly or indirectly, by a terrorist(s).

The term "designated persons" refers to those persons or entities designated by the Al-Qaida and Taliban Sanctions Committee pursuant to S/RES/1267(1999) or those persons or entities designated and accepted, if appropriate, by jurisdictions pursuant to S/RES/1373(2001).

The phrase "without delay," for the purposes of S/RES/1267(1999), means, ideally, within a matter of hours of a designation by the Al-Qaida and Taliban Sanctions Committee. For the purposes of S/RES/1373(2001), the phrase "without delay" means upon having reasonable grounds or a reasonable basis to suspect or believe that a person or entity is a terrorist, one who finances terrorism or a terrorist organization.

The phrase "without delay" should be interpreted in the context of the need to prevent the flight or dissipation of terrorist-linked funds or other assets, and the need for global, concerted action to interdict and disrupt their flow swiftly.

Freezing without delay terrorist related funds or other assets

In order to fulfill the preventive intent of Special Recommendation III, jurisdictions should establish the necessary authority and adopt the following standards and procedures to freeze the funds or other assets of terrorists those who finance terrorism and terrorist organizations in accordance with both S/RES/1267(1999) and S/RES/1373(2001):

Authority to freeze, unfreeze, and prohibit dealing in funds or other assets of designated persons. Jurisdictions should prohibit by enforceable means the transfer, conversion, disposition or movement of funds or other assets. Options for providing the authority to freeze and unfreeze terrorist funds or other assets include:
(i) empowering or designating a competent authority or a court to issue, administer and enforce freezing and unfreezing actions under relevant mechanisms, or
(ii) enacting legislation that places responsibility for freezing the funds or other assets of designated persons publicly identified by a competent authority or a court on the person or entity holding the funds or other assets and subjecting them to sanctions for noncompliance.

The authority to freeze and unfreeze funds or other assets should also extend to funds or other assets derived or generated from funds or other assets owned or controlled, directly or indirectly, by such terrorists, those who finance terrorism, or terrorist organizations.

Whatever option is chosen, there should be clearly identifiable competent authorities responsible for enforcing the measures.

The competent authorities shall ensure that their nationals or any persons and entities within their territories are prohibited from making any funds or other assets, economic resources or financial or other related services available, directly or indirectly, wholly or jointly, for the benefit of: designated persons, terrorists; those who finance terrorism; terrorist organizations; entities owned or controlled, directly or indirectly, by such persons or entities; and persons and entities acting on behalf of or at the direction of such persons or entities.

Freezing procedures. Jurisdictions should develop and implement procedures to freeze the funds or other assets specified in paragraph (c) below without delay and without giving prior notice to the persons or entities concerned. Persons or entities holding such funds or other assets should be required by law to freeze them and should furthermore be subject to sanctions for non-compliance with this requirement. Any delay between the official receipt of information provided in support of a designation and the actual freezing of the funds or other assets of designated persons undermines the effectiveness of designation by affording designated persons time to remove funds or other assets from identifiable accounts and places. Consequently, these procedures must ensure:

(i) the prompt determination whether reasonable grounds or a reasonable basis exists to initiate an action under a freezing mechanism and;

(ii) the subsequent freezing of funds or other assets without delay upon determination that such grounds or basis for freezing exist. Jurisdictions should develop efficient and effective systems for communicating actions taken under their freezing mechanisms to the financial sector immediately upon taking such action.

As well, they should provide clear guidance, particularly financial institutions and other persons or entities that may be holding targeted funds or other assets on obligations in taking action under freezing mechanisms.

Funds or other assets to be frozen or, if appropriate, seized. Under Special Recommendation III, funds or other assets to be frozen include those subject to freezing under S/RES/1267(1999) and S/RES/1373(2001). Such funds or other assets would also include those wholly or jointly owned or controlled, directly or indirectly, by designated persons. In accordance with their obligations under the United Nations International Convention for the Suppression of the Financing of Terrorism (1999) (the Terrorist Financing Convention (1999)), jurisdictions should be able to freeze or, if appropriate, seize any funds or other assets that they identify, detect, and verify, in accordance with applicable legal principles, as being used by, allocated for, or being made available to terrorists, those who finance terrorists or terrorist organizations. Freezing or seizing under the Terrorist Financing Convention (1999) may be conducted by freezing or seizing in the context of a criminal investigation or proceeding. Freezing action taken under Special Recommendation III shall be without prejudice to the rights of third parties acting in good faith.

De-listing and unfreezing procedures. Jurisdictions should develop and implement publicly known procedures to consider de-listing requests upon satisfaction of certain criteria consistent with international obligations and applicable legal principles and to unfreeze the funds or other assets of de-listed persons or entities in a timely manner. For persons and entities designated under S/RES/1267(1999), such procedures and criteria should be in accordance with procedures adopted by the Al-Qaida and Taliban Sanctions Committee under S/RES/1267(1999).

Unfreezing upon verification of identity. For persons or entities with the same or similar name as designated persons who are inadvertently affected by a freezing mechanism, jurisdictions should develop and implement publicly known procedures to unfreeze the funds or other assets of such persons or entities in a timely manner upon verification that the person or entity involved is not a designated person.

Providing access to frozen funds or other assets in certain circumstances. Where jurisdictions have determined that funds or other assets, which are otherwise subject to freezing pursuant to the obligations under S/RES/1267(1999), are necessary for basic expenses for the payment of certain types of fees, expenses, and service charges or for extraordinary expenses, [7] jurisdictions should authorize access to such funds or other assets in accordance with the procedures set out in S/RES/1452(2002) and subject to approval of the Al-Qaida and Taliban Sanctions Committee. On the same grounds, jurisdictions may authorize access to funds or other assets if freezing measures are applied pursuant to S/RES/1373(2001).

Remedies. Jurisdictions should provide for a mechanism through which a person or an entity that is the target of a freezing mechanism in the context of terrorist financing can challenge that measure with a view to having it reviewed by a competent authority or a court.

Sanctions. Jurisdictions should adopt appropriate measures to monitor effectively the compliance with relevant legislation, rules or regulations governing freezing mechanisms by financial institutions and other persons or entities that may be holding funds or other assets as indicated in paragraph 8(c) above. Failure to comply with such legislation, rules or regulations should be subject to civil, administrative, or criminal sanctions.

Seizure and Confiscation

Consistent with FATF Recommendation 3, jurisdictions should adopt measures similar to those set forth in Article V of the United Nations Convention against Illicit Traffic in Narcotic Drugs and Psychotropic Substances (1988), Articles 12 to 14 of the United Nations Convention on Transnational Organized Crime (2000), and Article 8 of the Terrorist Financing Convention (1999), including legislative measures, to enable their courts or competent authorities to seize and confiscate terrorist funds or other assets.

Footnotes:

When issued, S/RES/1267(1999) had a time limit of one year. A series of resolutions have been issued by the United Nations Security Council (UNSC) to extend and further refine provisions of S/RES/1267(1999). By successor resolutions are meant those resolutions that extend and are directly related to the original resolution S/RES/1267(1999). At the time of issue of this Interpretative Note, these resolutions included S/RES/1333(2000), S/RES/1363(2001), S/RES/1390(2002), and S/RES/1455(2003). In this Interpretative Note, the term

S/RES/1267(1999) refers to S/RES/1267(1999) and its successor resolutions.

For instance, both the United Nations Convention against Illicit Traffic in Narcotic Drugs and Psychotropic Substances (1988) and United Nations Convention against Transnational Organised Crime (2000) contain obligations regarding freezing, seizure, and confiscation in the context of combating transnational crime. Those obligations exist separately and apart from obligations that are set forth in S/RES/1267(1999), S/RES/1373(2001), and Special Recommendation III.

When the UNSC acts under Chapter VII of the UN Charter, the resolutions it issues are mandatory for all United Nations members.

The UNSC was acting under Chapter VII of the UN Charter in issuing S/RES/1373(2001) (see previous footnote).

Confiscation or forfeiture orders are usually linked to a criminal conviction or a court decision whereby the confiscated or forfeited property is determined to have been derived from or intended for use in a violation of the law.

A terrorist act includes an act which constitutes an offence within the scope of, and as defined in one of the following treaties: Convention for the Suppression of Unlawful Seizure of Aircraft, Convention for the Suppression of Unlawful Acts against the Safety of Civil Aviation, Convention on the Prevention and Punishment of Crimes against Internationally Protected Persons, including Diplomatic Agents, International Convention against the Taking of Hostages, Convention on the Physical Protection of Nuclear Material, Protocol for the Suppression of Unlawful Acts of Violence at Airports Serving International Civil Aviation, supplementary to the Convention for the Suppression of Unlawful Acts against the Safety of Civil Aviation, Convention for the Suppression of Unlawful Acts against the Safety of Maritime Navigation, Protocol for the Suppression of Unlawful

Acts against the Safety of Fixed Platforms located on the Continental Shelf, International Convention for the Suppression of Terrorist Bombings, and the International Convention for the Suppression of the Financing of Terrorism (1999).

Interpretative Note to Special Recommendation VI: Alternative Remittance

General

Money or value transfer systems have shown themselves vulnerable to misuse for money laundering and terrorist financing purposes. The objective of Special Recommendation VI is to increase the transparency of payment flows by ensuring that jurisdictions impose consistent anti-money laundering and counter-terrorist financing measures on all forms of money/value transfer systems, particularly those traditionally operating outside the conventional financial sector and not currently subject to the FATF Recommendations. This Recommendation and Interpretative Note underscore the need to bring all money or value transfer services, whether formal or informal, within the ambit of certain minimum legal and regulatory requirements in accordance with the relevant FATF Recommendations.

Special Recommendation VI consists of three core elements: Jurisdictions should require licensing or registration of persons (natural or legal) that provide money/value transfer services, including through informal systems;

    a. Jurisdictions should ensure that money/value transmission services, including informal systems (as described in paragraph 5 below), are subject to applicable FATF Forty Recommendations (in particular, Recommendations 10-21 and 26-29) and the Eight Special Recommendations (in particular Special Recommendation VII); and

Jurisdictions should be able to impose sanctions on money/value transfer services, including informal systems, that operate without a license or registration and that fail to comply with relevant FATF Recommendations.

Scope and Application

For the purposes of this recommendation, the following definitions are used:

"Money or value transfer service" refers to a financial service that accepts cash, cheques, other monetary instruments, or other stores of value in one location and pays a corresponding sum in cash or other form to a beneficiary in another location by means of a communication, message, transfer or through a clearing network to which the money/value transfer service belongs. Transactions performed by such services can involve one or more intermediaries and a third party final payment.

A money or value transfer service may be provided by persons (natural or legal) formally through the regulated financial system or informally through non-bank financial institutions or other business entities or any other mechanism either through the regulated financial system (for example, use of bank accounts) or through a network or mechanism that operates outside the regulated system. In some jurisdictions, informal systems are frequently referred to as alternative remittance services or underground (or parallel) banking systems. Often these systems have ties to particular geographic regions and are therefore described using a variety of specific terms. Some examples of these terms include *hawala*, *hundi*, *fei-chien*, and the black market peso exchange [1].

Licensing means a requirement to obtain permission from a designated competent authority in order to operate a money/value transfer service legally.

Registration in this recommendation means a requirement to register with or declare to a designated competent authority the existence of a money/value transfer service in order for the business to operate legally.

The obligation of licensing or registration applies to agents. At a minimum, the principal business must maintain a current list of agents which must be made available to the designated competent authority. An agent is any person who provides money or value transfer service under the direction of or by contract with a legally registered or licensed remitter (for example, licensees, franchisees, concessionaires).

Applicability of Special Recommendation VI

Special Recommendation VI should apply to all persons (natural or legal), who conduct for or on behalf of another person (natural or legal) the types of activity described in paragraphs four and five above as a primary or substantial part of their business or when such activity is undertaken on a regular or recurring basis, including as an ancillary part of a separate business enterprise.

Jurisdictions need not impose a separate licensing / registration system or designate another competent authority in respect to persons (natural or legal) already licensed or registered as financial institutions (as defined by the FATF Forty Recommendations) within a particular jurisdiction, which under such license or registration are permitted to perform activities indicated in paragraphs four and five above and which are already subject to the full range of applicable obligations under the FATF Forty Recommendations (in particular, Recommendations ten to twenty-one and twenty-six to twenty-nine) and the Eight Special Recommendations (in particular Special Recommendation VII).

Licensing or Registration and Compliance

Jurisdictions should designate an authority to grant licenses and or carry out registration and ensure that the requirement is observed. There should be an authority responsible for ensuring compliance by money/value transfer services with the FATF Recommendations (including the Eight Special Recommendations). There should also be effective systems in place for monitoring and ensuring such compliance. This interpretation of Special Recommendation VI (i.e., the need for designation of competent authorities) is consistent with FATF Recommendation twenty-six.

Sanctions

Persons providing money/value transfer services without a license or registration should be subject to appropriate administrative, civil, or criminal sanctions.[2] Licensed or registered money/value transfer services which fail to comply fully with the relevant measures called for in the FATF Forty Recommendations or the Eight Special Recommendations should also be subject to appropriate sanctions.

Footnotes:

The inclusion of these examples does not suggest that such systems are legal in any particular jurisdiction. Jurisdictions may authorize temporary or provisional operation of money / value transfer services that are already in existence at the time of implementing this Special Recommendation to permit such services to obtain a license or to register.

Revised Interpretative Note to Special Recommendation VII: Wire Transfers [1]

Objective

Special Recommendation VII was developed with the objective of preventing terrorists and other criminals from having unfettered access to wire transfers for moving their funds and for detecting such misuse when it occurs. Specifically, it aims to ensure that basic information on the originator of wire transfers is immediately available:

(1) to appropriate law enforcement and/or prosecutorial authorities to assist them in detecting, investigating, prosecuting terrorists, or other criminals and tracing the assets of terrorists or other criminals;

(2) to financial intelligence units for analyzing suspicious or unusual activity and disseminating it as necessary, and

(3) to beneficiary financial institutions to facilitate the identification and reporting of suspicious transactions.

Due to the potential terrorist financing threat posed by small wire transfers, countries should aim for the ability to trace all wire transfers and should minimise thresholds taking into account the risk of driving transactions underground. It is not the intention of the FATF to impose rigid standards or to mandate a single operating process that would negatively affect the payment system. The FATF will continue to monitor the impact of Special Recommendation VII and conduct an assessment of its operation within three years of full implementation.

Definitions

For the purposes of this interpretative note, the following definitions apply:

The terms "wire transfer" and "funds transfer" refer to any transaction carried out on behalf of an originator person (both natural and legal) through a financial institution by electronic means with a view to making an amount of money available to a beneficiary person at another financial institution. The originator and the beneficiary may be the same person.

"Cross-border" transfer means any wire transfer where the originator and beneficiary institutions are located in different countries. This term also refers to any chain of wire transfers that has at least one cross-border element.

"Domestic transfer" means any wire transfer where the originator and beneficiary institutions are located in the same country. This term therefore refers to any chain of wire transfers that takes place entirely within the borders of a single country, even though the system used to effect the wire transfer may be located in another country.

The term "financial institution" is as defined by the FATF Forty Recommendations (2003) [2]. The term does not apply to any persons or entities that provide financial institutions solely with message or other support systems for transmitting funds [3].
The originator is the account holder, or where there is no account, the person (natural or legal) who places the order with the financial institution to perform the wire transfer.

Scope
Special Recommendation VII applies, under the conditions set out below, to cross-border and domestic transfers between financial institutions.

Cross-border wire transfers

Cross-border wire transfers should be accompanied by accurate and meaningful originator information. However, countries may adopt a de minimus threshold (no higher than USD or EUR 1,000). For cross-border transfers below this threshold:
Countries are not obligated to require ordering financial institutions to identify, verify record, or transmit originator information.

Countries may nevertheless require that incoming cross-border wire transfers contain full and accurate originator information.

Information accompanying qualifying cross-border wire transfers [4] must always contain the name of the originator and where an account exists, the number of that account. In the absence of an account, a unique reference number must be included. Information accompanying qualifying wire transfers should also contain the address of the originator. However, countries may permit financial institutions to substitute the address with a national identity number, customer identification number, or date and place of birth. Where several individual transfers from a single originator are bundled in a batch file for transmission to beneficiaries in another country, they shall be exempted from including full originator information provided they include the originator's account number or unique reference number (as described in paragraph eight), and the batch file contains full originator information that is fully traceable within the recipient country

Domestic wire transfers
Information accompanying domestic wire transfers must also include originator information as indicated for cross-border wire transfers, unless full originator information can be made avail-

able to the beneficiary financial institution and appropriate authorities by other means. In this latter case, financial institutions need only include the account number or a unique identifier provided that this number or identifier will permit the transaction to be traced back to the originator.

The information must be made available by the ordering financial institution within three business days of receiving the request either from the beneficiary financial institution or from appropriate authorities. Law enforcement authorities should be able to compel immediate production of such information.

Exemptions from Special Recommendation VII
Special Recommendation VII is not intended to cover the following types of payments:

Any transfer that flows from a transaction carried out using a credit or debit card so long as the credit or debit card number accompanies all transfers flowing from the transaction. However, when credit or debit cards are used as a payment system to effect a money transfer, they are covered by Special Recommendation VII, and the necessary information should be included in the message.

Financial institution-to-financial institution transfers and settlements where both the originator person and the beneficiary person are financial institutions acting on their own behalf.
Role of ordering, intermediary, and beneficiary financial institutions

Ordering financial institution
The ordering financial institution must ensure that qualifying wire transfers contain complete originator information. The ordering financial institution must also verify this information for accuracy and maintain this information in accordance with the standards set out in the FATF Forty Recommendations (2003) [5].

Intermediary financial institution

For both cross-border and domestic wire transfers, financial institutions processing an intermediary element of such chains of wire transfers must ensure that all originator information that accompanies a wire transfer is retained with the transfer.

Where technical limitations prevent the full originator information accompanying a cross-border wire transfer from remaining with a related domestic wire transfer (during the necessary time to adapt payment systems), a record must be kept for five years by the receiving intermediary financial institution of all the information received from the ordering financial institution.

Beneficiary financial institution

Beneficiary financial institutions should have effective risk-based procedures in place to identify wire transfers lacking complete originator information. The lack of complete originator information may be considered as a factor in assessing whether a wire transfer or related transactions are suspicious and, as appropriate, whether they are thus required to be reported to the financial intelligence unit or other competent authorities. In some cases, the beneficiary financial institution should consider restricting or even terminating its business relationship with financial institutions that fail to meet SRVII standards.

Enforcement mechanisms for financial institutions that do not comply with wire transfer rules and regulations

Countries should adopt appropriate measures to monitor effectively the compliance of financial institutions with rules and regulations governing wire transfers. Financial institutions that fail to comply with such rules and regulations should be subject to civil, administrative, or criminal sanctions.

Footnotes:

It is recognized that countries will need time to make relevant legislative or regulatory changes and to allow financial institutions to make necessary adaptations to their systems and procedures. This period should not extend beyond December 2006.

When this Interpretative Note was originally issued, these references were to the 1996 FATF Forty Recommendations. Subsequent to the publication of the revised FATF Forty Recommendations in June 2003, this text was updated accordingly. All references are now to the 2003 FATF Forty Recommendations.

However, these systems do have a role in providing the necessary means for the financial institutions to fulfill their obligations under Special Recommendation VII and in particular, in preserving the integrity of the information transmitted with a wire transfer.

Throughout this Interpretative Note, the phrase "qualifying cross-border wire transfers" means those cross border wire transfers above any applicable threshold as described in paragraph four.

Interpretative Note to Special Recommendation VIII: Non-Profit Organizations

Introduction

Non-profit organizations (NPOs) play a vital role in the world economy and in many national economies and social systems. Their efforts complement the activity of the governmental and business sectors in providing essential services, comfort, and hope to those in need around the world. The ongoing international campaign against terrorist financing has unfortunately demonstrated however that terrorists and terrorist organizations exploit the NPO sector to raise and move funds, provide logistical support, encourage terrorist recruitment, or otherwise support terrorist organizations and operations. This misuse not only facilitates terrorist activity but also undermines donor confidence and jeopardizes the very integrity of NPOs. Therefore, protecting the NPO sector from terrorist abuse is both a critical component of the global fight against terrorism and a necessary step to preserve the integrity of NPOs.

NPOs may be vulnerable to abuse by terrorists for a variety of reasons. NPOs enjoy the public trust, have access to considerable sources of funds, and are often cash-intensive. Furthermore, some NPOs have a global presence that provides a framework for national and international operations and financial transactions often within or near those areas that are most exposed to terrorist activity. Depending on the legal form of the NPO and the country, NPOs may often be subject to little or no governmental oversight (for example, registration, record keeping, reporting, and monitoring) or few formalities may be required for their creation (for example, there may be no skills or starting capital required, no background checks necessary for employees). Terrorist organizations have taken advantage of these characteristics of NPOs to infiltrate the sector and misuse NPO funds and operations to cover for or support terrorist activity.

Objectives and General Principles
The objective of Special Recommendation VIII is to ensure that NPOs are not misused by terrorist organizations:
(i) to pose as legitimate entities;
(ii) to exploit legitimate entities as conduits for terrorist financing, including for the purpose of escaping asset freezing measures or;
(iii) to conceal or obscure the clandestine diversion of funds intended for legitimate purposes but diverted for terrorist purposes.
In this Interpretative Note, the approach taken to achieve this objective is based on the following general principles:
Past and ongoing abuse of the NPO sector by terrorists and terrorist organizations requires countries to adopt measures both:
(i) to protect the sector against such abuse and;
(ii) to identify and take effective action against those NPOs that either are exploited by or actively support terrorists or terrorist organizations.

Measures adopted by countries to protect the NPO sector from terrorist abuse should not disrupt or discourage legitimate charitable activities. Rather, such measures should promote transparency and engender greater confidence in the sector across the donor community and with the general public that charitable funds and services reach intended legitimate beneficiaries. Systems that promote achieving a high degree of transparency, integrity, and public confidence in the management and functioning of all NPOs are integral to ensuring the sector cannot be misused for terrorist financing.

Measures adopted by countries to identify and take effective action against NPOs that either are exploited by or actively support terrorists or terrorist organizations should aim to prevent and prosecute as appropriate terrorist financing and other forms of terrorist support. Where NPOs suspected of or implicated in terrorist financing or other forms of terrorist support are identified, the first priority of countries must be to investigate and halt such terrorist financing or support.

Actions taken for this purpose should, to the extent reasonably possible, avoid any negative impact on innocent and legitimate beneficiaries of charitable activity. However, this interest cannot excuse the need to undertake immediate and effective actions to advance the immediate interest of halting terrorist financing or other forms of terrorist support provided by NPOs.

Developing co-operative relationships among the public, private, and NPO sector is critical to raising awareness and fostering capabilities to combat terrorist abuse within the sector. Countries should encourage the development of academic research on and information sharing in the NPO sector to address terrorist financing related issues.

A targeted approach in dealing with the terrorist threat to the NPO sector is essential given the diversity within individual national sectors, the differing degrees to which parts of each sector may be vulnerable to misuse by terrorists, the need to ensure that legitimate charitable activity continues to flourish, and the limited resources and authorities available to combat terrorist financing in each jurisdiction.

Flexibility in developing a national response to terrorist financing in the NPO sector is also essential in order to allow it to evolve over time as it faces the changing nature of the terrorist financing threat.

Definitions

For the purposes of Special Recommendation VIII and this interpretative note, the following definitions apply:

The term "non-profit organization" or NPO refers to a legal entity or organization that primarily engages in raising or disbursing funds for purposes such as charitable, religious, cultural, educational, social, or fraternal purposes, or for the carrying out of other types of "good works."

The terms "FIU," "legal arrangement," and "legal person" are as defined by the FATF Forty Recommendations (2003) (the FATF Recommendations).

The term "funds" is as defined by the Interpretative Note to FATF Special Recommendation II.

The phrase "freezing terrorist and terrorist organization" is as defined by the Interpretative Note to FATF Special Recommendation III.

The term "appropriate authorities" refers to competent authorities, self-regulatory bodies, accrediting institutions, and other administrative authorities.

The term "beneficiaries" refers to those natural persons or groups of natural persons who receive charitable, humanitarian, or other types of assistance through the services of the NPO.

Measures

Countries should undertake domestic reviews of their NPO sector or have the capacity to obtain timely information on its activities, size, and other relevant features. In undertaking these assessments, countries should use all available sources of information in order to identify features and types of NPOs, which by virtue of their activities or characteristics, are at risk of being misused for terrorist financing. [1]Countries should also periodically reassess the sector by reviewing new information on the sector's potential vulnerabilities to terrorist activities.

There is a diverse range of approaches in identifying, preventing, and combating terrorist misuse of NPOs. An effective approach, however, is one that involves all four of the following elements:
(a) Outreach to the sector;
(b) Supervision or monitoring;
(c) Effective investigation and information gathering; and
(d) Effective mechanisms for international co-operation.

The following measures represent specific actions that countries should take with respect to each of these elements in order to protect their NPO sector from terrorist financing abuse.
a. Outreach to the NPO sector concerning terrorist financing issues:
(i) Countries should have clear policies to promote transparency, integrity, and public confidence in the administration and management of all NPOs.
(ii) Countries should encourage or undertake outreach programs to raise awareness in the NPO sector about the vulnerabilities of NPOs to terrorist abuse and terrorist financing risks and the measures that NPOs can take to protect themselves against such abuse.
(iii) Countries should work with the NPO sector to develop and refine best practices to address terrorist financing risks and vulnerabilities and thus protect the sector from terrorist abuse. [2]
(iv) Countries should encourage NPOs to conduct transactions via regulated financial channels, wherever feasible, keeping in mind the varying capacities of financial sectors in different countries and in different areas of urgent charitable and humanitarian concerns.
b. Supervision or monitoring of the NPO sector
Countries should take steps to promote effective supervision or monitoring of their NPO sector. In practice, countries should be able to demonstrate that the following standards apply to NPOs which account for (1) a significant portion of the financial re-

sources under control of the sector and (2) a substantial share of the sector's international activities.

(i) NPOs should maintain information on:

(1) the purpose and objectives of their stated activities and;

(2) the identity of the person(s) who own, control, or direct their activities, including senior officers, board members, and trustees. This information should be publicly available either directly from the NPO or through appropriate authorities.

(ii) NPOs should issue annual financial statements that provide detailed breakdowns of incomes and expenditures.

(iii) NPOs should be licensed or registered. This information should be available to competent authorities. [3]

(iv) NPOs should have appropriate controls in place to ensure that all funds are fully accounted for and are spent in a manner that is consistent with the purpose and objectives of the NPOs stated activities.

(v) NPOs should follow a "know your beneficiaries and associate NPOs [4]" rule, which means that the NPO should make best efforts to confirm the identity, credentials and good standing of their beneficiaries and associate NPOs. NPOs should also undertake best efforts to document the identity of their significant donors and to respect donor confidentiality.

(vi) NPOs should maintain, for a period of at least five years, and make available to appropriate authorities records of domestic and international transactions that are sufficiently detailed to verify that funds have been spent in a manner consistent with the purpose and objectives of the organization. This also applies to information mentioned in paragraphs (i) and (ii) above.

(vii) Appropriate authorities should monitor the compliance of NPOs with applicable rules and regulations. [5] Appropriate authorities should be able to properly sanction relevant violations by NPOs or persons acting on behalf of these NPOs. [6]

c. Effective information gathering and investigation

(i) Countries should ensure effective co-operation, co-ordination, and information sharing to the extent possible among all levels of appropriate authorities or organizations that hold relevant information on NPOs.

(ii) Countries should have investigative expertise and capability to examine those NPOs suspected of either being exploited by or actively supporting terrorist activity or terrorist organizations.

(iii) Countries should ensure that full access to information on the administration and management of a particular NPO (including financial and programmatic information) may be obtained during the course of an investigation.

(iv) Countries should establish appropriate mechanisms to ensure that when there is suspicion or reasonable grounds to suspect that a particular NPO:

(1) is a front for fundraising by a terrorist organization;

(2) is being exploited as a conduit for terrorist financing, including for the purpose of escaping asset freezing measures; or

(3) is concealing or obscuring the clandestine diversion of funds intended for legitimate purposes but redirected for the benefit of terrorists or terrorist organizations, this information is promptly shared with all relevant competent authorities in order to take preventative or investigative action.

d. Effective capacity to respond to international requests for information about a NPO of concern

Consistent with Special Recommendation V, countries should identify appropriate points of contact and procedures to respond to international requests for information regarding particular NPOs suspected of terrorist financing or other forms of terrorist support.

Footnotes:

For example, such information could be provided by regulators, tax authorities, FIUs, donor organizations, or law enforcement and intelligence authorities.

The FATF's Combating the Abuse of Non-Profit Organizations: International Best Practices provides a useful reference document for such exercises.

Specific licensing or registration requirements for counter terrorist financing purposes are not necessary. For example, in some countries, NPOs are already registered with tax authorities and monitored in the context of qualifying for favorable tax treatment (such as tax credits or tax exemptions).

The term "associate NPOs" includes foreign branches of international NPOs.

In this context, rules and regulations may include rules and standards applied by self-regulatory bodies and accrediting institutions.

The range of such sanctions might include freezing of accounts, removal of trustees, fines, de-certification, de-licensing, and de-registration. This should not preclude parallel civil, administrative, or criminal proceedings with respect to NPOs or persons acting on their behalf where appropriate.

Interpretative Note to Special Recommendation IX: Cash Couriers

Objectives
FATF Special Recommendation IX was developed with the objective of ensuring that terrorists and other criminals who cannot finance their activities or launder the proceeds of their crimes through the physical cross-border transportation of currency and bearer negotiable instruments. Specifically, it aims to ensure that countries have measures:
1) to detect the physical cross-border transportation of currency and bearer negotiable instruments;
2) to stop or restrain currency and bearer negotiable instruments that are suspected to be related to terrorist financing or money laundering;
3) to stop or restrain currency or bearer negotiable instruments that are falsely declared or disclosed;
4) to apply appropriate sanctions for making a false declaration or disclosure and;
5) to enable confiscation of currency or bearer negotiable instruments that are related to terrorist financing or money laundering.
Countries should implement Special Recommendation IX sub-

ject to strict safeguards to ensure proper use of information and without restricting either:
(i) trade payments between countries for goods and services or;
(ii) the freedom of capital movements in any way.

Definitions
For the purposes of Special Recommendation IX and this Interpretative Note, the following definitions apply:

The term "bearer negotiable instruments" includes monetary instruments in bearer form such as: traveller's cheques; negotiable instruments (including cheques, promissory notes, and money orders) that are either in bearer form, endorsed without restriction, made out to a fictitious payee, or otherwise in such form that title thereto passes upon delivery; incomplete instruments (including cheques, promissory notes, and money orders) signed but with the payee's name omitted.[1]

The term "currency" refers to banknotes and coins that are in circulation as a medium of exchange.

The term "physical cross-border transportation" refers to any inbound or out-bound physical transportation of currency or bearer negotiable instruments from one country to another country. The term includes the following modes of transportation:
(1) physical transportation by a natural person or in that person's accompanying luggage or vehicle;
(2) shipment of currency through containerized cargo or;
(3) the mailing of currency or bearer negotiable instruments by a natural or legal person.

The term "false declaration" refers to a misrepresentation of the value of currency or bearer negotiable instruments being transported or a misrepresentation of other relevant data which is asked for in the declaration or otherwise requested by the authorities. This includes failing to make a declaration as required.

The term "false disclosure" refers to a misrepresentation of the value of currency or bearer negotiable instruments being transported, or a misrepresentation of other relevant data asked for in the disclosure or otherwise requested by the authorities. This includes failing to make a disclosure as required.

When the term related to terrorist financing or money laundering is used to describe currency or bearer negotiable instruments, it refers to currency or bearer negotiable instruments that are:
(i) the proceeds of, or used in, or intended or allocated for use in, the financing of terrorism, terrorist acts, or terrorist organizations; or
(ii) laundered proceeds from money laundering, or predicate offences, or instrumentalities used in or intended for use in the commission of these offences.

The types of systems that may be implemented to address the issue of cash couriers

Countries may meet their obligations under Special Recommendation IX and this Interpretative Note by implementing one of the following types of systems; however, countries do not have to use the same type of system for incoming and outgoing cross-border transportation of currency or bearer negotiable instruments:

Declaration system: The key characteristics of a declaration system are as follows. All persons making a physical cross-border transportation of currency or bearer negotiable instruments, which are of a value exceeding a pre-set, maximum threshold of EUR/USD 15,000, are required to submit a truthful declaration to the designated competent authorities. Countries that implement a declaration system should ensure that the pre-set threshold is sufficiently low to meet the objectives of Special Recommendation IX.

Disclosure system: The key characteristics of a disclosure system are as follows:

All persons making a physical cross-border transportation of currency or bearer negotiable instruments are required to make a truthful disclosure to the designated competent authorities upon request. Countries that implement a disclosure system should ensure that the designated competent authorities could make their inquiries on a targeted basis based on intelligence or suspicion, or on a random basis.

Additional elements applicable to both systems:
Whichever system is implemented, countries should ensure their system incorporates the following elements:

The declaration/disclosure system should apply to both incoming and outgoing transportation of currency and bearer negotiable instruments.

Upon discovery of a false declaration/disclosure of currency or bearer negotiable instruments or a failure to declare/disclose them, designated competent authorities should have the authority to request and obtain further information from the carrier with regard to the origin of the currency or bearer negotiable instruments and their intended use.

Information obtained through the declaration/disclosure process should be available to the financial intelligence unit (FIU) either through a system whereby the FIU is notified about suspicious cross-border transportation incidents or by making the declaration/disclosure information directly available to the FIU in some other way.

At the domestic level, countries should ensure that there is adequate co-ordination among customs, immigration, and other related authorities on issues related to the implementation of Special Recommendation IX.

In the following two cases, competent authorities should be able to stop or restrain cash or bearer negotiable instruments for a reasonable time in order to ascertain whether evidence of money laundering or terrorist financing may be found:
(i) where there is a suspicion of money laundering or terrorist financing; or
(ii) where there is a false declaration or false disclosure.
The declaration/disclosure system should allow for the greatest possible measure of international co-operation and assistance in accordance with Special Recommendation V and Recommendations thirty-five to forty. To facilitate such co-operation, in instances when:
(i) a declaration or disclosure which exceeds the maximum threshold of EUR/USD 15,000 is made, or
(ii) where there is a false declaration or false disclosure or;
(iii) where there is a suspicion of money laundering or terrorist financing, this information shall be retained for use by the appropriate authorities.
At a minimum, this information will cover:
(i) the amount of currency or bearer negotiable instruments declared or disclosed or otherwise detected; and
(ii) the identification data of the bearer(s).

Sanctions
Persons who make a false declaration or disclosure should be subject to effective, proportionate, and dissuasive sanctions, whether criminal, civil, or administrative. Persons who are carrying out a physical cross-border transportation of currency or bearer negotiable instruments that are related to terrorist financing or money laundering should also be subject to effective, proportionate, and dissuasive sanctions, whether criminal, civil, or administrative and should be subject to measures, including legislative ones consistent with Recommendation three and Special Recommendation III, which would enable the confiscation of such currency or bearer negotiable instruments.

Footnotes:

For the purposes of this Interpretative Note, gold, precious metals, and precious stones are not included despite their high liquidity and use in certain situations as a means of exchange or transmitting value. These items may be otherwise covered under customs laws and regulations. If a country discovers an unusual cross-border movement of gold, precious metals, or precious stones, it should consider notifying, as appropriate, the Customs Service or other competent authorities of the countries from which these items originated and/or to which they are destined and should co-operate with a view toward establishing the source, destination, and purpose of the movement of such items and towards the taking of appropriate action.

References

1. Sterling, Claire. *Crime without frontiers: the worldwide expansion of organized crime and the Pax Mafiosa.*
2. Arab News, August 19th 2003
3. Woods, Brett F. *Art and Science of Money Laundering.* 1998
4. Retter, Terry, and Ray Seddigh. *Anti-Money Laundering.*
5. Nakajima, Chizu V., and Barry A.K. Rider. *Anti-Money laundering Guide: Fixed Network.*
6. Reuter, Peter. *Chasing Dirty Money: Progress on Anti-Money laundering.* 2003
7. Nakajima, Chizu V., and Barry A.K. Rider. *Anti-Money Laundering Guide: Academic/International Network*
8. Hyde, Lorraine. *Bank Secrecy Act and Anti-Money Laundering Service.* R.S.M McGladrey. 1996
9. United States compendium of selected anti-money laundering statutes and rules, United States Dept. of Treasury.
10. US anti-money laundering law for 2001
11. United Nations Convention Against Illicit Traffic in Narcotic Drugs and Psychotropic Substances, 1988
12. FATF Forty Recommendations and Nine Special Recommendations

http://www.globalcorruptionreport.org
http://www1.oecd.org/media/release/hrmfltaxbriefingpaper.pdf
http://www.oecd.org/
http://www.imf.org/
http://www.un.org/
http://www.interpol.int/
http://www.fatf-gafi.org/pages/0,2966,en_32250379_3223572
0_1_1_1_1_1,00.html
http://www.uic.it/en/antiriciclaggio-en/altro_en/UE_1991_06
_10.htm
http://www.cbe.org.eg/
http://www.whitehousedrugpolicy.gov/about/index.html
http://untreaty.un.org/English/Terrorism/Conv12.pdf
http://www.imf.org/external/pubs/ft/fandd/2002/12/elqorchi.htm
http://www.worldbank.org/
http://www.wolfsberg-principles.com/
http://www.treas.gov/offices/eotffc/ofac/
http://www.ustreas.gov/irs/ci/articles/docblackmarketpeso.htm
http://www.state.gov/g/inl/rls/nrcrpt/2001/rpt/
http://www.incb.org/e/conv/1988/